Economy and Environment

ECONOMY AND ENVIRONMENT

A Theoretical Essay on the Interdependence of Economic and Environmental Systems

Charles Perrings
University of Auckland

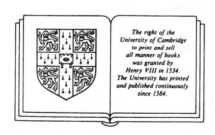

The right of the
University of Cambridge
to print and sell
all manner of books
was granted by
Henry VIII in 1534.
The University has printed
and published continuously
since 1584.

CAMBRIDGE UNIVERSITY PRESS

Cambridge

New York   Port Chester   Melbourne   Sydney

CAMBRIDGE UNIVERSITY PRESS
Cambridge, New York, Melbourne, Madrid, Cape Town, Singapore, São Paulo

Cambridge University Press
The Edinburgh Building, Cambridge CB2 2RU, UK

Published in the United States of America by Cambridge University Press, New York

www.cambridge.org
Information on this title: www.cambridge.org/9780521340816

First published 1987
Reprinted 1990
This digitally printed first paperback version 2005

A catalogue record for this publication is available from the British Library

Library of Congress Cataloguing in Publication data
Perrings, Charles.
  Economy and environment.
    1. Economic development – Environmental aspects.
I. Title.
HD75.6.P47   1987   333.7   87–18329

ISBN-13 978-0-521-34081-6 hardback
ISBN-10 0-521-34081-0 hardback

ISBN-13 978-0-521-02076-3 paperback
ISBN-10 0-521-02076-X paperback

TO ARISTIDES AND HARITINI, KIPARISSIA

Contents

vii

Preface

This book studies the dynamic implications of the links between the economy and its environment. In many disciplines, an examination of the relation between a referent system and the physical medium in which it exists – grows, stagnates, or contracts – would require no justification. In most anthropological models, for example, the environment is omnipresent. However, it is remarkable how unimportant the environment is in the eyes of most economists. The scarcity of resources, the raison d'être of the discipline, is founded on the limited supply of resources in a finite world. Yet in almost every formal model of the economic system, the environment has no meaningful role to play. This remains true despite the burgeoning literature on resource depletion and environmental pollution over the past two decades. These remain specialized and isolated branches of economics with little or no impact on the mainstream of economic theory, even though there is by now a popular awareness that there must eventually be an end to human rapacity and waste.

The essay has been written against the background of an assurgent economic liberalism that is carrying almost all before it. Cutting a swathe through a diverse literature on external effects, property rights, transaction costs, welfare, and growth, it has given rise to an environmental strategy called here the market solution. The three legs of this strategy are the sovereignty of the individual, the sanctity of private property, and the domination of the present. Its effect is to justify the abdication of our collective responsibility for the outcome of our actions. Although it supposes that we can see and even make our own future, the strategy generates increasing uncertainty and myopia. It may believe that we can resolve the conflicts of interest arising out of unexpected environmental effects by the simple act of allocating property rights and establishing contingent markets, yet it generates ever more pressing sources of dispute.

By exploring the time behavior of a jointly determined economy-environment system, this essay tackles the theoretical implications of the environmental blindness that underpins the formal foundations of the market solution. Building on the one set of economic models that makes a serious attempt to explain the implications of the drive to accumulation in modern economies, the classical growth models, it seeks to establish just what the price mechanism can be expected to do in an economy-environment system and what it cannot. The classical growth models are not, however, the only sources tapped. Indeed, the essay has roots in a very disparate set of contributions to a wide range of debates. Some – those within economics in particular – are discussed explicitly. Others are present only as implicit influences. Because they have been important influences, however, it is worth making at least a general acknowledgment of their contribution. The anthropological literature on primitive economies has been a fruitful source of comparative insights into the management of economy-environment relations – as will be made clear. Similarly, the historical work on ancient and feudal economic systems in Europe has proved very suggestive, as have the classical and Marxian debates on the nature of accumulation in the periphery of the world economy – at the interface between capitalist and noncapitalist forms of production. Since the environment to an economy may include human as well as nonhuman systems of production, coercive systems of production such as the slave, feudal, or corvee systems are directly analogous to the more familiar exploitation of nonhuman environments. For this reason, the debates on the dynamics of such systems have been particularly illuminating.

More directly, the essay is a response to the now very numerous American contributions to the economics of the environment, and particularly to the original work on mass-balance systems by Ayres, d'Arge, and Kneese. These have added a great deal of importance to our understanding of the links between economy and environment. They have brought the environment to center stage in at least one branch of economics, and have raised important questions about the environmental assumptions ordinarily made in economic theory. At the same time, however, because most of the works building on the foundations laid by the mass-balance models have been unable to escape the trap of static neoclassical allocation theory, they have failed to address the crucially important implications of the conservation of mass for the time behavior of the system.

It will be apparent to even the most casual reader that I owe a considerable intellectual debt to Georgescu-Roegen. Not only has he tackled many of the same problems, but his penetrating remarks on the parallel time behavior of material and energy systems have provided a central reference point for the essay. He might not approve its arguments, and he is certainly not responsible for its deficiencies, but without his pioneering studies I could not have begun to ask many of the questions most central to the book.

In addition, I am indebted to a number of individuals and institutions whose support has sustained the effort required to produce the work. The University of Auckland has provided both an environment conducive to work of this sort, and most of the financial support needed to carry it out. To colleagues Geoffrey Braae, Kenneth Jackson, and Martin O'Connor I am grateful for various fruitful discussions. To Shula Marks and members of the seminars of the Institute of Commonwealth Studies, University of London, where much of the preliminary work was done with the support of a Henry Chapman Fellowship, I owe such understanding as I have of primitive economies. Alan Rogers provided a valuable testing ground for the logic of the arguments advanced, although the usual disclaimer applies. Walter Birmingham brought a fund of experience and common sense to his comments on earlier drafts. Donald Katzner made very helpful comments at various stages in the development of the work. I have also benefited from the comments of the editors and readers of the journals in which preliminary results have been published, from E. K. Hunt who read the manuscript, and from the patient and insightful suggestions of Colin Day of Cambridge University Press.

Notation guide

Because the basic arguments of this book are developed mathematically, and since this involves frequent use of notation, the following guide is provided for ease of reference. Uppercase bold letters denote matrices, lowercase bold letters denote vectors, and lowercase roman and Greek letters denote scalars. Columns within a matrix are denoted by an indexed, lowercase, bold letter. Rows within a matrix are denoted by an indexed, lowercase, bold letter with a horizontal bar below. Symbols that are time indexed are followed by a scalar, usually k, in brackets.

$\mathbf{A}(k)$ = a gross input coefficient matrix
$\mathbf{A}_\Delta(k)$ = a gross input coefficient change matrix
$\mathbf{B}(k)$ = a net output coefficient matrix
$\mathbf{B}_\Delta(k)$ = a net output coefficient change matrix
$\mathbf{e}$ = the unit vector
$\mathbf{I}$ = the identity matrix
$\mathbf{j}(k)$ = a row vector of control variables
$\mathbf{J}(k)$ = a controllability matrix
$\mathbf{k}(k)$ = a column vector of control system outputs
$\mathbf{K}(k)$ = an observability matrix
$\mathbf{M}(k)$ = a feedback matrix
$\mathbf{p}(k)$ = a column vector of prices
$\mathbf{q}(k)$ = a row vector of resource quantities
$\mathbf{q}_R(k)$ = a row vector of residual quantities
$\mathbf{q}_E(k)$ = a row vector of excess demands
$\mathbf{r}(k)$ = a column vector of process revenues
$\mathbf{u}(k)$ = a column vector of unemployment rates
$\mathbf{v}(k)$ = a column vector of investment rates
$\mathbf{w}(k)$ = a column vector of rents
$\mathbf{X}(k)$ = a gross input matrix
$\mathbf{y}(k)$ = a column vector of net incomes
$\mathbf{Z}(k)$ = a net output matrix

CHAPTER 1

Introduction

1.1 The problem of external effects

From the innocent parable of the bees to the poisonous gas clouds of Bhopal, environmental external effects are evidence of the price system's inability to signal the true significance of the interdependence of human activities undertaken within a common environment. They are the ex-post measures of the environmental effects of activities launched in a state of deliberate or accidental blindness as to their consequences. Although external effects are all-pervasive, it is by no means universally accepted that they constitute a significant "problem" for economic theory. Like the social costs of racism or sexism, external effects are not susceptible to exact estimation precisely because they are outside the price system, and whether one believes them to be significant is often argued to depend on one's ideological predisposition. This book seeks to demonstrate that environmental external effects represent fundamental flaws in the axiomatic structure of the dominant models of the economic system, and that the adoption of an appropriate axiomatic structure changes the properties of those models in an important way. More particularly, it alters both the conceptualization of the environmental management problem and the criteria for developing strategies to deal with it.

The modern theory of external effects stems from two seminal articles in the early 1950s by Meade (1952) and Scitovsky (1954). These articles established that the basis of external effects is the nonindependence of the preference and production functions of economic agents who operate within a common environment, but who do not meet in the marketplace. To Meade, we owe the useful distinction between external effects that are the product of the direct interdependence of producers or consumers, which he called "unpaid factors of production," and those that are the product of indirect interdependence, which he termed "creation of atmosphere." To Scitovsky, we owe the suggestion that time and uncertainty are key ingredients in the generation of external effects. The importance of both the directness of the interdependence of economic processes and the link between time and uncertainty will be recurrent themes in this work.

Ironically, although later authors declared themselves receptive to the explanation of the causes of external effects offered in these two articles, they have typically drawn a rather different set of inferences. Meade's recommended use of Pigouvian taxes and subsidies, and Scitovsky's implicit judgments as to the weighting of social over private rates of time preference in the face of uncertainty, have both fallen foul of the assurgent economic liberalism that underpins the currently dominant environmental strategy – the "market solution." Increasingly, the emphasis is on internalizing external effects through the allocation of property rights. Uncertainty is interpreted as risk, and so reduced to a problem in the theory of probability. The distinction between the time perspective of the collectivity and that of its individual members is trivialized, and the role allowed the collectivity whittled away.

This would cause no difficulty if it were not for the fact that the market solution can be shown to generate only increasing turbulence and uncertainty, a progressive myopia, and a heightened risk of conflict. By exploring the general problem of the time behavior of a jointly determined economy-environment system, this essay shows why. By probing the significance of time in our perceptions of the global system, it demonstrates that the positive discounting of the uncertainty of the future can lead only to greater uncertainty. The market solution exaggerates the very problem it is designed to remedy.

What is ultimately at issue are the properties of an environmental strategy that is duly sensitive to the physical constraints on economic activity, to the existence of uncertainty in the sense of Knight (1921), Shackle (1955), and Georgescu-Roegen (1971), to the limitations of the price system, and to the ethical imperative for being aware of the needs of future generations. This takes us into a very wide-ranging set of debates, initiated as early as 1848 with John Stuart Mill's *Principles,* and touching on problems in the theory of growth, time, uncertainty, welfare, depletion, and pollution. It asks us to rethink the questions raised by the Club of Rome report, *The Limits to Growth,* which were buried in the welter of accusations and counteraccusations that followed its publication in 1972. It asks that we pay closer attention to the extraordinarily suggestive work of Georgescu-Roegen, usually shrugged off by those who prefer to ignore the physical foundations of economic activity. Most important, it asks us to reconsider the fundamental environmental assumptions underpinning our theories of the time behavior of economic systems.

The problem of external effects exists because something has been left out or distorted in the description of the essential elements of reality summarized in the axiomatic structure of our models. Recognition that the problem may be significant is at once recognition that our models may be significantly flawed. Hence, the defensiveness of those who deny the significance of external effects is defensiveness over the "correctness" of the particular world view contained in the axiomatic structure of their models.

All deductive theory is necessarily limited by what may loosely be called the framework within which the arguments are worked out. This framework is given by the axiomatic structure on which the propositions of the theory are established. Since the propositions in deductive theory add nothing to the axioms and merely draw out their implications, the axiomatic structure or framework of the theory establishes the range of possible results. Hence, by selecting one set of axioms over another it is possible to ensure one set of results rather than another. The axioms of a theory in a very real sense contain its conclusions. The results on the existence and uniqueness of equilibrium in the dynamic models of general economic equilibrium turn out to be highly sensitive to the assumptions made about the role of the environment. Yet few assumptions of the general equilibrium models are challenged less frequently than those relating to the environment.

1.2   The environment in economic theory

Consider the identification of the economy and its environment. At the most general level, a human economy may be defined as a physical system of production organized according to a social system of signals. As a first approximation, we may define a physical system of production to be a mutually dependent set of material transformations, or processes, designed to yield a particular set of services. We may define a social system of signals to be a set of mutually consistent indicators recognizable to and guiding the behavior of a particular society. In the idealized market economy of theoretical economics the processes of the physical system are organized according to a very particular system of signals – the price system. In the "primitive" economies and, indeed, in most economies of the real world, the system of signals is invariably a composite of exchange values and a range of cultural or ideological codes of behavior. In all cases, though, it is the system of signals that sets an economy apart from the other systems of social production with which it interacts.

Nor is the economy unique in this respect. All forms of social production comprise a set of processes that, in principle at least, can be defined by the system of signals informing the behavior of the agents operating those processes. In other words, a system of social production contains all those processes controlled by reference to the relevant social signals. Because of the interdependence of systems of social production, however, it follows that one system of signals may overlap another. Indeed, the human economy is founded on activities that depend on the ability of human agents to manage the signals guiding the behavior of agents in other (subordinate) systems of production. if these signals are not controllable, then the outputs flowing from a well-defined combination of inputs may not be predictable. The material transformations that are the point of such activities may not be determinate.

The limit of human control in such circumstances marks the dividing line between the economy and its environment. Hence, if the agents of an economy are able to control all systems of production, no environment will exist. The environment may be said to be completely dominated by that economy. Conversely, if the agents of an economy are unable to control any system of production, that economy may be said to be completely dominated by its environment. In all cases it is notionally possible to describe the global physical system in terms of a referent system of production and its environment. The concept of an environment is thus very general. If we take the set of all the material transformations undertaken in the general system at a given moment in time to be the universal set and denote this by U, and if we define the material transformations of a given (referent) system of production, $O \subset U$, to be a subset of the universal set, then the complement of the referent set, $O^* \subset U$, is the environment of that set. Symmetrically, if O^* is the referent set, O is its environment.

Consider the environmental assumptions generally made in economic theory. It is worth noting at the outset that there is a marked difference between the environmental assumptions common to the majority of theories of the modern capitalist economy and those common to both anthropological theories of primitive economies and physiocratic theories of early-modern economies. The last two generally suppose the economy to be dominated by its environment, the former generally believe that the economy dominates its environment. The assumption of the dominant economy comes in two versions. The first may be called the *weak environmental assumption*. It supposes that an environment exists; that it is not completely dominated by the economy, but that it plays only a benign and passive role. The second may be called the *strong environmental assumption*. It supposes that the economy completely dominates its environment. It is tantamount to an assumption that an environment does not exist.

The weak environmental assumption is of older lineage, as one might expect. It represents a transitional assumption, a compromise between the assumption of a dominant environment made by the Physiocrats, and the assumption of a dominant economy that appears in at least one modern general equilibrium theory. The weak environmental assumption first appeared in the work of the classical political economists, but was not stated with any clarity until Marx's *Capital*. In this work we find the claim that "those things which labour merely separates from immediate connexion with their environment are subjects of labour spontaneously provided by Nature. Such are fish which we catch and take from their element, water, timber which we fell in the virgin forest, and ores which we extract from their veins" (1954, p. 174). They are the *free gifts* of the environment. The production process was, for Marx, a problem of environmental control, in which "man of his own accord starts, regulates, and controls the material reactions between himself and Nature. . . . Thus Nature becomes one of the organs of his activity, one that he annexes to his own bodily organs, adding stature to himself in spite of the Bible" (ibid., pp. 173–5).

The assumption of free gifts is one-half of the weak environmental assumption. The counterpart to the assumption of free gifts was not formally acknowledged until much later, although it is now standard in the dynamic general equilibrium models evolved in the wake of Neumann's classic (1945–6) paper. Not only is it assumed that the economy may expand without limit at the expense of its environment, it is also assumed that the economy can dispose costlessly of unlimited quantities of waste material within its environment. The environment is simultaneously a horn of plenty and a bottomless sink. The weak environmental assumption means both the assumption of free gifts and the assumption of the *free disposal* of wastes. The physical system under the weak environmental assumption may be represented by a description of all processes using or producing commodities, and only those processes. The environment need not be represented since it does not constrain the system except occasionally or incidentally. The mass of the output of the system may either expand or contact, since any matter required for new output may be freely obtained from the environment and any waste may be freely disposed of in the environment.

The strong environmental assumption is a later addition to the literature. It is never made explicit, and is tenable only under the powerful assumption that the system is static. A system of production under this assumption is, in the words of the title of Sraffa's famous book, a system of *Production of Commodities by Means of Commodities*. All processes are controlled by agents responding to the price system. As we will see, change involving an increase or decrease in the mass of output implies the existence of some source of mass or some waste receptacle other than the economy. Indeed, if a system of production of commodities by means of commodities is rendered dynamic, it can neither expand nor contract. It is only if the system is assumed to be timeless that this does not matter.

In contrast to the strong environmental assumption, the weak environmental assumption allows the claim that a model encompasses all those effects of the interaction of economy and environment that are economically relevant, given the time horizon of the analysis. The environment may induce a degree of uncertainty, but the conventional argument since Debreu (1959) is that this may be accommodated ex ante by pricing for risk. If unforeseen but economically relevant effects do occur, then the argument developed by Coase (1960) is that these so-called external effects may be accommodated ex post through the allocation of property rights, without disturbing the basic assumptions of the resource allocative models. Environmental external effects are treated as an occasional or incidental problem. It is assumed that the environment is generally controllable, but that where the limits of environmental control are exceeded, the resulting of unforeseen costs or benefits accruing to agents in the economy can be negotiated away by the allocation of appropriate property rights.

The selective appeal to reality associated with the axiomatic structure of the dominant economic models is not without its critics. From a deductivist perspective Kornai (1972) has made a swingeing assault on the validity of a science that betrays such a cavalier attitude to the reality it is supposed to explain in the selection of its axiomatic foundations. From an inductivist perspective Leontief (1971) has condemned an approach that deliberately eschews the discipline of empirical verification. On the particular matter of the environmental assumptions of general equilibrium theory, the exclusion of the natural environment has been challenged in the numerous contributions that followed the work of Boulding (1966), Daly (1968), Ayres and Kneese (1969), Georgescu-Roegen (1971), d'Arge (1972), and the Club of Rome (Meadows et al., 1972).

Given the overwhelming empirical evidence that the natural environment does have a major impact on the economy that is not captured by the price system, the raison d'être of such work is readily intelligible. It is remarkable, however, how little effect it has had on economic theorists. This may be because the intellectual problem is much deeper than an awareness of the human propensity to foul the natural environment. Once we begin to conceptualize the behavior of economy-environment systems over time, unprotected by the assumption that the price system contains all the information we need to know, we find not the comfortable order of stable or relatively stable equilibria but a seemingly chaotic drive to change, paralleled only in the recent findings of physicists investigating the time behavior of structures far from equilibrium (cf. Prigogine and Stengers, 1977). More important, we observe little warrant for the simple Smithian faith in the invisible hand that underpins the market solution, and no warrant at all for the argument that forward markets will compel private interests to secure the information that renders the price system complete.

1.3   Toward a constructive theory of economy-environment interactions

The arguments of this essay are developed in discrete stages, with each corresponding to a different level of abstraction. Part I explores the time behavior of indecomposable physical systems bound by the laws of thermodynamics. The fundamental problem here is that alluded to by Meade: the significance of the physical interdependence of processes via some medium or environment. The analysis abstracts from the complications brought about by the social institutions and signaling system of the economy. It is concerned solely with the time behavior of physical systems. The importance of this in the general argument lies in that fact that the economic system, like any other system of production, rests on physical foundations. It must behave in a way that is consistent with physical laws. It is not, as the free gifts and free disposals assumptions would have it, exempt from those laws.

When working with the limited range of variables admitted at a high level of abstraction, it is convenient to draw out the implications of a particular set of assumptions mathematically. Part I develops a formal model to explore the dynamic behavior of a jointly determined economy-environment system that shares certain features with what has become a broad genus of economy-environment models based on the extension of the basic linear input-output model. Cumberland (1966), Daly (1968), Leontief (1970), Victor (1972) and Lipnowski (1976) have all produced models of this type. The most important feature shared with such models is the assumption, first made in the context of a general equilibrium model by Ayres and Kneese (1969), that a closed physical system must satisfy the conservation of mass condition. As Boulding had pointed out to economists in his celebrated 1966 paper, for all practical purposes matter can be neither created nor destroyed. The mass of resources potentially available for exploitation in the global system, or in any isolated part of the global system, is the same now as it was a million years ago.

Although the assumption of the conservation of mass is relaxed at points in this essay to consider the properties of particular subsystems within the general system, it represents the single most important general assumption of the work. Its implications are far from trivial. Interestingly, it is perhaps the least important of these implications that has attracted the most popular attention: the fact that the growth of any technologically stationary economic system will inevitably run that system up against Malthusian limits. By contrast, the most important implication has been almost completely neglected. It is the necessity for any system generating residuals in the process of production to change over time, to evolve from one state to the next as the residuals generated in production are returned to the system in either a controlled or uncontrolled way.

The traditional free gifts and free disposal assumptions deny both implications. If these assumptions are made, it is necessary to consider neither the limits to growth nor the evolutionary nature of the system. It is of some interest, therefore, that the free gifts and free disposal assumptions have been cornerstones in the development of the theory of the time behavior of economic systems. Only by ignoring the physical foundations of economic systems has it been possible to generalize the static equilibrium results of the Walrasian system to the dynamic case: to pretend to the relevance of equilibrium growth in a technologically stationary world. Neumann's (1945–6) model of general equilibrium, for example, proved to be of seminal importance in developing the theory of economic dynamics, yet it was built on an extraordinarily powerful set of assumptions about the ability of an economy to function independently of its environment. Although it was a remarkable tour de force in terms of the theoretical insights it yielded about the equilibrium growth properties of certain types of system, it was not even an approximate description of the environmentally open economies of the real world. The fact that it was subsequently treated as such – particularly by the string of contributions on the "turnpike" (cf. Turnovsky, 1970, and Tsukui and Marakami, 1979) – is evidence of the casual disregard for the validity of the assumptions of equilibrium models so vehemently criticized by Kornai. For theories based on deductive inference to yield practically relevant results (as opposed to abstract ideological goals), the axioms of those theories must correspond to the essential features of the real systems being modeled. Since the results of all equilibrium models of economic behavior are obtained by deductive inference on the axioms or assumptions of the models, they must satisfy these requirements to be taken seriously as explanations of reality. If they do not, these models can have the status of experiments only.

The difficulty with the traditional environmental assumptions is naturally most acute in dynamic models. Since the free gift and free disposal assumptions turn out to fail before the feedback effects of residual disposals in an indecomposable economy environment system, they are unsustainable except where such feedback effects are assumed to be too distant to be relevant. This may be a valid assumption in a static allocation problem (if it is ever legitimate to abstract from time in economic problems), but it cannot be so in any general dynamic model of economic behavior. If we are interested in the development of economic systems over time, we simply cannot ignore the effects of residual disposals other than controlled investment.

Accordingly, while the model developed here shares certain features of the Neumann model, it is not constrained by the same environmental assumptions. Instead, it explores the significance of the conservation of mass condition for the time behavior of jointly determined economy-environment systems without prejudging the ability of one to override the other. Moreover, the system is shown to be time varying. Although it shares the fixed production coefficient assumption of both the Neumann growth model and the input-output environmental models, it does not assume a static technology. Production coefficients are fixed only in the sense that the inherited technology in a given period will be embodied in a set of physical assets that bear a fixed proportion of one another. In a time-varying system those coefficients will change from period to period.

More important, perhaps, the conventional notion that there exists an initially complete book of blueprints from which are drawn the techniques of production applied in all future periods is argued to be untenable. This does not mean that there is no choice of technique, merely that choice of technique is not the only source of technological change. Future allocations in a jointly determined economy-environment system turn out to be unknowable in advance. Each allocation is the unique and unreproducible outcome of the disposal of a set of residuals that is beyond the control of the agents of any one subsystem.

I do not, therefore, begin with commodity production, the near universal starting point for theories resting on either the strong or the weak environmental assumption. I begin with production in general, where this refers to the material transformations undertaken by all agents in the system irrespective of their species. It represents the highest level of abstraction. I do not suggest that any real-world system of production is not specific to the time and place in which it occurs, but that it is useful to consider the elements that different systems of production have in common. In no other way can we see how the material tranformations of one system may limit those of another, regardless of differences in the rules of the game in each.

Part II considers the structure of the price system, and the role of prices in signaling resource scarcity. Once again, the properties of the price system depend on the fact that I seek to describe the time behavior of a jointly determined economy-environment system. To this I add the supposition that the system is subject to contest over both the appropriation of property (in resolution of external effects) and the distribution of returns to property (in sympathy with the classical models). The price system is assumed not only to ration a given set of resources at a given moment in time, but to discriminate between resources that are subject to rights in property and those that are not, and to mediate the conflicting claims to the social product of distinct classes of economic agent. It thus admits a broader set of functions than is common in models built on strictly neoclassical foundations and allows a less restrictive set of outcomes.

In this sense the economy-environment model developed here contrasts with the Ayres and Kneese (1969) model – one of the earliest and most original attempts to examine the implications for general economic equilibrium of the conservation of mass. Since the authors locked themselves into an essentially static allocative (Walras–Cassel) framework in which they assumed the existence of a stable equilibrium, they blinkered themselves against the most significant implication of the conservation of mass: the nonexistence of stable economic equilibria. The powerful equilibrium orientation of the static allocative models in the Walrasian mold makes them, in these circumstances, unhelpful. Indeed, the economic problem addressed – the problem of economic growth in a far-from-equilibrium, time-varying, economy-environment system subject to the conservation of mass – is much closer to that addressed by the classical political economists than by their neoclassical successors. The classical problem was, as Walsh and Gram put it, "the capacity of an economy to reproduce itself and grow" (1980, p. 9). This is very different from the optimal allocation of given resources addressed by Walras. Consequently, although I wish to construct a dynamic model of general economic (dis)equilibrium, it is to the classical and not the neoclassical general equilibrium theories that I appeal. In other words, I consider a model that builds on the work of Smith, Ricardo, and Marx, and not that of Walras.

Because the physical system described here is a jointly determined economy-environment one, it depicts the behavior over time of a vector of resources, some of which have the status of *commodities* and some of which do not. Commodities in such a system imply resources that have value in exchange and are subject to well-defined rights of property. They include not only products in the usual sense of the word, but also labor and any valorized resource extracted from the environment. This is not, it should be emphasized, an unusual approach. As Makarov and Rubinov explain, "the word 'products' is . . . interpreted in a broad sense in mathematical models of economics. The set of 'products' does not only contain products in the normal sense of the word, but also contains various types of labour, natural resources and various types of 'conditional' products (i.e., products whose quantities measure the effect of some other products)" (1977, p. 59). The processes undertaken by households are registered in exactly the same way as the processes undertaken by any other institution, just as in the Leontief (1971) general equilibrium model. What is unusual is the inclusion in the model of *environmental resources:* those that do not have the status of commodities. Such resources are not valorized – they lie outside the price system of the economy.

Far from demonstrating the stable equilibrium properties of the price system, the analysis points to the necessity for that system to be driven from one disequilibrium state to the next by persistent external effects that result from the unobservability and uncontrollability of the processes of the environment through the price system. Moreover, the effect of contest over the distribution of property (assets) and income is shown to exacerbate the time variability of the system. The problem of external effects turns out to be an inevitable and integral part of a system in which resources exist that are uncontrolled by economic agents, where control is a function of possession rather than property – of the ability to influence the output of the resource in question through the application of valorized inputs, rather than through legal title.

Part III addresses the problem of optimal environmental strategies in an evolutionary world. The core of the problem is argued to be uncertainty: not the probabilistic uncertainty that assumes away our inability to foresee the effects of our actions, but uncertainty before ignorance, novelty, and surprise. This uncertainty follows from the system's existence in real, historical, irreversible time. It is the uncertainty that is at once the unifying thread in all Shackle's works, and the counterpart to the irreversibility of thermodynamic processes argued with such persistence by Georgescu-Roegen. It is argued in this book that the only means of dealing with this type of uncertainty is by discounting it, and that this is, in fact, the real basis of the market solution to the twin environmental problems of depletion and pollution.

This directs our attention to the critical importance of time preference and to the distinction between the private rate of time preference (authorized by private property) and the social rate of time preference (authorized by common property). It is argued that the microeconomic optimal depletion and pollution theories underpinning the market solution depend on assumptions made about time preference, while ignoring the existence of positive feedbacks between rates of time preference, uncertainty, and external effects. More particularly, it is argued that, unlike the traditional Pigouvian approach to depletion and pollution policy, the market solution depends on the assumption of the dominance of the private over the social rate of time preference. The market solution is the antithesis of the quiescent environmental strategies associated with the primitive economies and supported by the modern proponents of the stationary state from John Stuart Mill to Herman Daly. Whereas the primitive economies rest on the institution of common property and the dominance of social over private rates of time preference, advocates of the market solution assume the primacy of both private property and the individual perspective on time.

1.4   "Old wine, new wineskins"

There is nothing in this book that is not to be found, in one guise or another, in the contributions of the various authors who have addressed the issues it raises; and there is little that might not be distilled from a sensitive reading of the works of Georgescu-Roegen. At the same time, however, no one has teased out the implications of the different strands of thought offered in this literature. Perhaps this is because so much is at stake. By pretending what Shackle calls the "omnicompetence" of humanity, economists have been able to wish away the problem of real uncertainty, to assert the sufficiency of economic signals and the irrelevance of unsignalled effects, and to equate property with control. It has been possible to offer the ex-ante optimizing models of economic theory as somehow "better" sources of guidance than the augury common in primitive economies. In the presence of pervasive external effects, however, such models necessarily lose much of their determinacy. Given uncertainty, the choice algo-rithms of optimizing models turn out to be very weak guides to human behavior. The environment and the uncertainty it brings are not just awkward complications. They are the Scylla and Charybdis of eco-nomic theory.

This essay is about old problems and old worries. It is nearly a hundred years now since Sidgwick linked time preference to the uncer-tainty of human existence. The alarm bells rung by the Club of Rome report to warn of the impending exhaustion of fossil fuels had been sounded over a hundred years before by Stanley Jevons. The problem of population pollution had concerned economists even before the publication of Malthus's *Essay* in 1798, and the question of the com-patibility of private and public interest has been an issue with moral philosophers since Plato. What is offered here is a new perspective on an old set of problems, based on a new look at the axiomatic structure of our models of the time behavior of economic systems. By changing the theoretical framework, it has been possible to change the light in which we see both the problems and the efficacy of their various solu-tions. It may be that the impetuousness of the market solution is itself irreversible, but if it is not, and if it is possible to alert at least some to the implications of the progressive myopia that comes with rising uncertainty, the exercise will have been worthwhile.

PART I

The physical economy-environment system

CHAPTER 2

Closed physical systems: a model

2.1 Elements of the system

A central characteristic of the major models of economic growth – the Neumann, Leontief, and Solow-Samuelson models – is that they are constructed on the basis of a description of the physical conditions of production. The set of production possibilities determines what is argued to be of interest in such models: the equilibrium state of the system and the stability or relative stability of that state. The description of the material transformations of the general economy-environment system discussed below diverges in a number of very fundamental ways from these models, but it rests on the same conviction that the dynamics of economic systems depend on the physical conditions of production. The axiomatic framework of a model of a dynamic economic system should include a stylized description of these conditions. This is what Fuss and McFadden (1978) have called "the traditional starting point of production theory." It is instructive that they and other proponents of duality theory have since abandoned such an approach on the grounds that economic data allegedly contain all the information relevant to the analysis of production. As we will see, however, the conditions of production remain the only credible basis for the analysis of economic systems unprotected by the free gifts and free disposals assumptions, and managed according to a set of signals as incomplete as the set of prices turns out to be.

The assumptions discussed here are, accordingly, assumptions about the physical conditions of production. It will become immediately apparent that these assumptions reflect a rather different view of the physical world from that commonly adopted in multisector economic growth models. The physical system described here is not the isolated and environmentally unimportant set of economic processes conventionally assumed in these models. Consequently, the model discussed here has none of the traditional safeguards against the effects of pollution, exhaustion, or unpredictable technological change. More important, the physical system is not deterministic. A knowledge of the initial conditions is not sufficient to give a knowledge of the time path of the system. Indeed, the system generates the very uncertainty that has blunted economists' interest in the theory of growth.

The system described here comprises both economy and environment, although at this stage the distinction between them is unimportant. The assumptions discussed here concern the nature of production in general, not the productive activities undertaken by particular groups of agents. In other words, they characterize the general properties of the material transformations of the global physical system. This focus on the global system is not without precedent. Over twenty years ago Boulding (1966) wrote about "The Economics of the Coming Spaceship Earth." Two years later Herman Daly published a paper in which he insisted on the importance and relevance of "interrelations whose connecting links are external to the economists' abstract world of commodities but very much internal to the world in which we live, move and have our being" (1968, p. 400). The conceptualization of the time behavior of the global system offered here is far removed from Daly's adaptation of the static Leontief model, but both are founded on the notion that economic analysis cannot be abstracted from the wider physical environment in which production takes place.

The essential characteristics of the global physical system may be summarized in the following five assumptions.

Assumption 1: The first and most fundamental assumption is that the global system is thermodynamically closed. To see what this means, note that physical systems may be classified in one of three ways according to the nature of their interaction with their surroundings. A system is said to be open if it exchanges both matter and energy with its environment. It is said to be closed if it exchanges energy but not matter with its environment. It is said to be isolated if it exchanges neither energy nor matter with its environment. The characterization of the global system as closed implies that it exchanges energy, such as radiant heat or gravity, with its environment, but is materially self contained. No matter can pass into or out of the system.

Since the model described here is one of material transformations, this is an important limiting assumption. Indeed, it is the source of the conservation of mass condition, on which many of the results of the work depend. Since matter can (for all practical purposes) be neither created nor destroyed, it means that all production in the global system involves the transformation of a fixed mass according to a set of more or less well-defined physical laws.

Assumption 2: The second assumption made here is that the global system is not decomposable, although at various points in this essay it will be useful to consider the properties of decomposable systems. The reason for this will be made clear late in this chapter. The assumption states that all subsystems within the global system, such as the human economy, are open with respect to their environments. We cannot identify closed subsystems within the global system. Both energy and matter pass between the processes of any subsystem, including the economy, and the environment. Hence, the processes of the economy are assumed to obtain raw materials from the environment and to deposit waste materials in the environment. Symmetrically, the processes of the environment are assumed to obtain raw materials from the economy and to deposit waste materials in the economy.

It is worth remarking now that it follows from *assumptions 1* and *2* that we cannot represent the material transformations of the economy as a closed system of the Sraffa (1960) type unless we assume that all material transformations in the whole system are controlled by economic agents. Although some authors have actually gone this far in recent years (Smith, 1977), the supposition is so manifestly unrealistic as to be discounted as a useful approximation of the present state of the global system.

Assumption 3: It is possible to describe the material transformations of the system over its history in terms of a finite number of activities or processes, each of which uses and generates a finite number of resources. More particularly, it is assumed that it is possible to identify the same number of processes and resources; that each resource is produced by at least one process; and that each process uses at least one resource. The number of resources produced and the number of processes undertaken may be expected to change over time. That is, the list of both useful and nonuseful or even dangerous resources may be expected to change. The number of processes undertaken during the history of the system will therefore by the sum of all processes undertaken during all periods in its history.

To clarify the next assumption, notice that the system of material flows described here supposes a system of energy flows, even though there is no explicit account of energy in the model. The material transformations of the system are driven by energy, and are therefore limited by the laws of thermodynamics. These laws underpin the relative scarcity of resources. Indeed, the value of productive resources is universally a function of entropy change – the "useful work" that they perform. In economic systems this useful work is synonymous with the concept of the services derived from either agents or assets. As Georgescu-Roegen puts it, "the Entropy Law is the taproot of economic scarcity. In a world in which that law did not operate, the same energy could be used over and over again at any velocity of circulation one pleased and material objects would never wear out. . . . In our world, everything that has some usefulness (desirability) for us consists of low entropy. It is for these reasons that the economic process is entropic in all its material fibres" (1979, p. 1041; see also 1971, 1973).

The explanation for this is that although energy may be neither created nor destroyed – by the First Law of thermodynamics, its availability for useful work is limited by the irreversability of entropic processes – the Second Law of thermodynamics. Any activity involving useful work entails an increase in the entropy of the system, and hence a decrease in the energy available for further useful work. Wood cannot be burned over and over again. The implications of the Second Law will be touched on at various points in this work. For now, however, what is important is what it tells us about the depreciation of productive resources.

Assumption 4: Consistent with the existence of high and low entropy states of matter, not all resources depreciate/degenerate at the same rate. This means that where processes use what the classical political economists called instruments of labor, the system will be one of joint production. The outputs of a particular process will include both new products and partially degraded instruments of production, alongside wastes equal to the difference between the mass of all inputs and the mass of these "valued" outputs. The simple production systems described by, for example, Sraffa (1960) and Leontief (1941) represent very special cases indeed.

Assumption 5: The set of material transformations undertaken in each period of the history of the system is characterized by fixed coefficients of production, implying constant returns to scale in all processes. The assumption of constant returns to scale dispenses with the need to make special assumptions about the period of production in different processes. This assumption is equivalent to the assumption of homogeneity of degree one made in various other growth models. Notice, though, that it is intended to reflect the fact that at any given moment in its history the system operates with an inherited technology embodied in a set of resources combined in given proportions. The world, defined in a given period, is not a tabula rasa, and its agents do not have complete freedom to determine the optimal combination of resources. They may change the combination of resources in subsequent periods – indeed they will be compelled to do so – but the coefficients of historically determined processes are fixed. The assumption of constant returns reflects the property of physical systems that they expand exponentially up to the point at which they are constrained by their environment. This property will be explored in detail in later chapters.

It will be apparent that while some of these assumptions are shared by other multisector growth models, the assumption that the physical system is thermodynamically closed, and is therefore subject to the law of conservation of mass, is not. It reflects the fact that I describe the economy-environment system, and not just the economic system. In the short period, the economic system, like any other subsystem of the global system, is not bound by the law of conservation of mass. That is, the physical mass of economically valued resources can expand at the expense of the environment. Eventually, however, the economy will run up against the constraints to growth imposed by the law of the conservation of mass.

2.2 Technology

In this book *technology* means the pool of knowledge that bounds all material transformations of the global system. It thus represents the sum of all the historically acquired chemical, genetic, intuitive, or recorded knowledge of material transformations. Technology accordingly means very much more than the science of the "industrial arts" in one or other historically specific human economy. The technology of the general system of the kth period of its history may be described by the pair of nonnegative matrices $A(k)$, $B(k)$. From *assumptions 2* to *5*, $A(k)$ and $B(k)$ are both n-square for all $k \geq 0$:

$$A(k) = \begin{bmatrix} a_{11}\, a_{12} \ldots a_{1n} \\ a_{21}\, a_{22} \ldots a_{2n} \\ \vdots \\ a_{n1}\, a_{n2} \ldots a_{nn} \end{bmatrix} (k) \qquad B(k) = \begin{bmatrix} b_{11}\, b_{12} \ldots b_{1n} \\ b_{21}\, b_{22} \ldots b_{2n} \\ \vdots \\ b_{n1}\, b_{n2} \ldots b_{nn} \end{bmatrix} (k)$$

2.1

In addition, $A(k)$ is indecomposable and $B(k)$ is not totally decomposable. $A(k)$ is the matrix of gross input coefficients, and $B(k)$ the matrix of net output coefficients (outputs net of depreciation), obtaining during the kth production period. The elements of $A(k)$ and $B(k)$ describe, respectively, the input requirements and the output possibilities of all processes in the system at unit activity levels. $\mathbf{a}_i(k)$, the ith row of $A(k)$, is the vector of gross input coefficients for the n resources of the system in the ith process in the kth period. $\mathbf{a}_j(k)$, the jth column of $A(k)$, is the vector of gross input coefficients for the jth resource in the n processes of the system in the kth period. $\mathbf{b}_i(k)$, the ith row of $\mathbf{B}(k)$, is the vector of net output coefficients for the n resources of the system in the ith process in the kth period. $\mathbf{b}_j(k)$, the jth column of $\mathbf{B}(k)$, is the vector of net output coefficients for the jth resource in the n processes of the system.

The $a_{ij}(k)$ and $b_{ij}(k)$ are input and output coefficients, respectively, on resources available to the system at the commencement of the reference period, and not on resources produced by the system in that period. They are not, therefore, Leontief coefficients. More particularly, $a_{ij}(k)$ denotes the gross input of the jth resource in the ith process per unit of the ith resource available to the system at the commencement of the kth period. Symmetrically, $b_{ij}(k)$ denotes the net output of the jth resource from the ith process per unit of the ith resource available to the system in the kth period. The difference between the two, $a_{ij}(k) - b_{ij}(k)$, indicates the growth (physical appreciation) or depreciation factor. If it is zero, the jth input to the ith process is unchanged in production in the kth period. If positive, the jth input is subject to partial depreciation. If negative, the jth input is augmented in production. If $a_{ij}(k) = 0$, but $b_{ij}(k) > 0$, then the jth output is a new product of the ith process.

To see the construction of these coefficients, let us define two further matrices, $\mathbf{X}(k)$, and $\mathbf{Z}(k)$, in which $x_{ij}(k)$ and $z_{ij}(k)$ denote, respectively, the gross input and the net output of the jth resource in the ith process in the kth period. $\mathbf{X}(k)$ and $\mathbf{Z}(k)$ are of similar dimension and sign to $\mathbf{A}(k)$ and $\mathbf{B}(k)$. Let us also define a nonnegative, time-indexed, n-dimensional row vector $\mathbf{q}(k)$.

$$\mathbf{q}(k) = [q_1 \, q_2 \ldots q_n](k) \qquad\qquad 2.2$$

in which $q_i(k)$ indicates the mass of the ith resource available to the system at the beginning of the kth period. If the ith resource is produced in the $k - 1$th period of the history of the system, $q_i(k) > 0$; if it is not produced, $q_i(k) = 0$. The coefficients $a_{ij}(k)$ and $b_{ij}(k)$ are thus defined by

$$a_{ij}(k) = q_i(k)^{-1} x_{ij}(k) \qquad b_{ij}(k) = q_i(k)^{-1} z_{ij}(k) \qquad 2.3$$

which subsume the activity level vectors of the classical multisector growth models.

In a technologically stationary system $\mathbf{A}(k) = \mathbf{A}(0)$ and $\mathbf{B}(k) = \mathbf{B}(0)$ for all $k \geq 0$. If the system is time varying, that is, technologically nonstationary, $\mathbf{A}(k) \neq \mathbf{A}(0)$ and $\mathbf{B}(k) \neq \mathbf{B}(0)$ for at least one $k > 0$. In a time-varying system, $\mathbf{A}(k) = \mathbf{A}(k - 1) + \mathbf{A}_\Delta (k - 1)$ and $\mathbf{B}(k) =$

$\mathbf{B}(k - 1) + \mathbf{B}_\Delta (k - 1)$, where $\mathbf{A}_\Delta (k - 1)$ and $\mathbf{B}_\Delta (k - 1)$ record changes in the coefficients of $\mathbf{A}(k - 1)$ and $\mathbf{B}(k) - 1)$ as the planned or unplanned result of the actions of the agents of the system. It follows that although $\mathbf{A}(k)$ and $\mathbf{B}(k)$ are nonnegative for all k, $\mathbf{A}_\Delta (k)$ and $\mathbf{B}_\Delta (k)$ are unrestricted as to sign. $a_{\Delta ij}(k)$ and $b_{\Delta ij}(k)$ may be greater than, equal to, or less than zero depending on whether the input or output coefficient of the jth resource in the ith process is augmented, unchanged, or diminished in the $k + 1$th period. For convenience, $\mathbf{A}(k)$ and $\mathbf{B}(k)$ will hereafter be referred to simply as the input and output matrices.

2.3 The conservation of mass and the "free gifts" of Nature

We may now begin to explore the technological implications of *assumption 1,* the assumption that the system is thermodynamically closed, and is therefore subject to the law of the conservation of mass. This draws on the arguments developed in Perrings (1986a). It is convenient to tackle the problem in stages, exploring the properties of the general model in the process. To begin with, consider the implications of the conservation of mass for the classical assumption that resources required in production are freely available in limitless quantities – the assumption of free gifts. Although it is intuitively obvious that the concepts of conservation of mass and free gifts are mutually inconsistent, it is worth establishing in what ways this inconsistency prescribes the technology of the system.

First, notice that $q_i(k)$ may be greater than, equal to, or less than $q_i(k + 1)$ for all k, implying that output of the ith resource may contract, remain unchanged, or expand from one period to the next. However, the conservation of mass condition means that the combined mass of all the $q_i(k)$, which we may write, using the unit or summing vector $\mathbf{e}$, as $\mathbf{q}(k)\mathbf{e}$, must be constant for all k. That is,

$$\mathbf{q}(k)\mathbf{e} = \mathbf{q}(k + 1)\mathbf{e} \qquad 2.4$$

for all $k \geq 0$.

Second, the mass of the outputs of any process in a given period must be equal to the mass of the inputs of that process. That is,

$$q_i(k)\underline{\mathbf{a}}_i(k)\mathbf{e} = q_i(k)\underline{\mathbf{b}}_i(k)\mathbf{e} \qquad 2.5$$

for all $k \geq 0$. This is a general interpretation of the dictum that nothing can be produced out of nothing. It is much stronger than the standard requirement of production functions of the form $Q = Q(\mathbf{x})$, that $Q(0) = 0$. Both 2.4 and 2.5 follow from the fact that in a closed system no matter may be added to the system from outside, and no matter may be ejected from the system. Notice, though, that 2.5 does not say that the mass of the economically valued inputs to a process should be equal to the mass of the economically valued outputs of that process. It says only that the mass of all inputs employed in a given process will be equal to the mass of all outputs produced by that process. If the mass of economically valued outputs of a process is less than the mass of inputs to the process, then the balance will be waste. This is, in fact, the main microeconomic implication of the material balance models of d'Arge, Ayres, and Kneese.

To see the systemic implications of 2.4 and 2.5, consider the time behavior of a system defined by a given technology at which all resources are fully employed in all periods and all resources are produced in positive quantities. This is tantamount to an assumption that the system is technologically stationary: that is, that $\mathbf{A}(k) = \mathbf{A}$, $\mathbf{B}(k) = \mathbf{B}$ for all $k \geq 0$. If this seems to be an unacceptably strong assumption, even for exploratory purposes, it is worth recalling that it is the standard assumption of all the major multisector growth models.

In all cases the outputs of the system in the kth period are given by the first-order difference equation:

$$q(k + 1) = q(k)\mathbf{B}(k) \qquad 2.6$$

That is, the stock of resources available to the system in the $k + 1$th period is the output of the system in the kth period. Because we are assuming that all resources are produced in positive quantities, $q_i(k) > 0$ for all i and all k. The significance of the full employment assumption is discussed in the next section. Here it is sufficient to note that it means that we can represent the time path of $q(k)$ without explicit reference to the input matrix $\mathbf{A}$. In the special case of a technologically stationary system the general solution of 2.6 is of the conveniently simple form:

$$q(k) = q(0)\mathbf{B}^k \qquad 2.7$$

This represents what may be called automatous behavior. The system automatically repeats the activities of the previous periods. The time path of $q(k)$ in such a system depends both on the values of the components of $q(0)$, and on the structure of $\mathbf{B}$. Suppose, for now, that the matrix $\mathbf{B}$ is indecomposable, implying that it is impossible to reduce it to a block diagonal or block triangular form. This means that it is impossible to identify any one sector producing a discrete set of outputs.

It is easy to see that as k tends to infinity, $q(k)$ is convergent or, more precisely, that $\mathbf{q}(k)$ tends to a left eigenvector of $\mathbf{B}$ corresponding to the dominant eigenvalue of $\mathbf{B},\lambda_{max}(\mathbf{B})$. Since $\mathbf{B}$ is a square nonnegative matrix it has a dominant eigenvalue: an eigenvalue that is real, positive, and greater in absolute value than all other eigenvalues. We may write the set of all the eigenvalues of $\mathbf{B}$ as the components of the vector $\lambda = [\lambda_1, \ldots, \lambda_n]$, and let these components be ordered such that $\lambda_{max} = \lambda_1$. There exists a nonsingular matrix S, and so a matrix $\mathbf{T} = \mathbf{S}^{-1}$, such that $\mathbf{B} = \mathbf{SD\lambda T}$, in which the first row of $\mathbf{T}$, $\underline{\mathbf{t}}_1$, and the first column of S, $\mathbf{s}_1$, are the left and right eigenvectors, respectively, of $\mathbf{B}$ corresponding to λ_1, and in which $\mathbf{D\lambda}$ is the diagonal matrix formed from the vector λ. That is,

$$\mathbf{D\lambda} \begin{bmatrix} \lambda_1 \, 0 \ldots 0 \\ 0 \, \lambda_2 \ldots 0 \\ \cdots\cdots\cdots \\ 0 \;\; 0 \ldots \lambda_n \end{bmatrix} \qquad\qquad 2.8$$

By the Frobenius theorem the components of $\underline{\mathbf{t}}_1$ and $\mathbf{s}_1$ are strictly positive; $\mathbf{B}$ is an indecomposable, nonnegative, square matrix. From 2.7 we have

$$\mathbf{q}(k) = \mathbf{q}(0)\mathbf{SD}\lambda^k\mathbf{T} \qquad\qquad 2.9$$

Multiplying both sides of 2.9 by λ_1^{-k} yields

$$\mathbf{q}(k)\lambda_1^{-k} = \mathbf{q}(0)\mathbf{SD}[\lambda_1^{-1}\lambda]^k\mathbf{T} \qquad\qquad 2.10$$

Since λ_1 is the dominant eigenvalue of $\mathbf{B}$, as k tends to infinity $[\lambda_1^{-k}\lambda]^k$ tends to $[1,0,\ldots,0]$. Consequently, we have, in the limit

$$\lim_{k\to\infty}\mathbf{q}(k)\lambda_1^{-k} = \mathbf{q}(0)\mathbf{SD}[1,0,\ldots,0]\mathbf{T} \qquad\qquad 2.11$$

Since $\mathbf{q}(0)\mathbf{SD}[1,0,\ldots,0]$ is a row vector that is positive in its first component only, while the first row of $\mathbf{T}$ is a strictly positive left eigenvector of $\mathbf{B}$, for k very large $\mathbf{q}(k)$ becomes very close to a left eigenvector of $\mathbf{B}$ corresponding to $\lambda_{max}(\mathbf{B})$.

If $\mathbf{B}$ is not indecomposable, it may be permuted to the form

$$\mathbf{B} = \begin{bmatrix} \mathbf{B}_{11} \; \mathbf{B}_{12} \\ \mathbf{0} \;\; \mathbf{B}_{22} \end{bmatrix} \qquad\qquad 2.12$$

in which the submatrices $\mathbf{B}_{11}$ and $\mathbf{B}_{22}$ are, respectively, m and $n - m$ square. If $\mathbf{q}(k)$ is partitioned conformably, that is,

$$\mathbf{q}(k) = [\mathbf{q}_1 \, \mathbf{q}_2](k) \qquad\qquad 2.13$$

such that $q_1(k)$ and $q_2(k)$ are m and $n - m$ dimensional vectors, respectively, it is clear that the time path of the first m resources in the system is entirely independent of the time path of the last $n - m$ resources. That is, we may write the general solution of the difference equations describing the time path of the first m resources in the form

$$q_1(k) = q_1(0)B_{11}^k \qquad\qquad 2.14$$

The time path of the last $n - m$ resources, on the other hand, depends on all processes in the system. That is, $q_2(k)$ is found in the solution to

$$[q_1 \ q_2](k) = [q_1 \ q_2](0) \begin{bmatrix} B_{11} & B_{12} \\ 0 & B_{22} \end{bmatrix}^k \qquad\qquad 2.15$$

Whether the first m processes of the system are in fact significant in the limit depends on the relative potential growth rates of the two subsystems. If the potential rate of growth of the subsystem described by B_{11} is greater than that of the subsystem described by B_{22}, then the dominant eigenvalue of B will be the dominant eigenvalue of the submatrix B_{11}. Conversely, if the potential rate of growth of the subsystem described by B_{22} is greater than that described by B_{11}, then the dominant eigenvalue of B will be the dominant eigenvalue of B_{22}. If the dominant eigenvalue of B is the dominant eigenvalue of B_{11}, then by a theorem of Gantmacher on reducible matrices (1959, p. 92ff), the left eigenvector of B corresponding to $\lambda_{max}(B)$ will be positive. But if the dominant eigenvalue of B is the same as the dominant eigenvalue of B_{22}, the left eigenvector of B corresponding to $\lambda_{max}(B)$ will be semipositive and zero in its first m components. This means that, in the limit, the first m processes will be significant in determining the magnitudes of the last $n - m$ resources only if the potential rate of growth of the first m resources is greater than the potential rate of growth of the last $n - m$ resources.

If B is indecomposable and $\lambda_{max}(B) > 1$, as k gets very large the system will get very close to an expansion path at which it will be growing exponentially, with all resources growing at the same rate. The same result will occur if B is decomposable and the dominant eigenvalues of both B_{11} and B_{22} have an absolute value greater than one. If B is indecomposable and $\lambda_{max}(B) < 1$, the system will collapse completely. The components of $q(k)$ will converge to zero. If B is decomposable, then it will be possible for one subsystem to collapse while the other expands exponentially.

The eventual rate of growth of an automatous system operating a given technology is therefore $\lambda_{\max}(\mathbf{B}) - 1$. The essential point here is that it is only if $\lambda_{\max}(\mathbf{B}) = 1$ in the indecomposable case, and if both $\lambda_{\max}(\mathbf{B}_{11}) = 1$ and $\lambda_{\max}(\mathbf{B}_{22}) = 1$ in the decomposable case, that the components of the vector $\mathbf{q}(k)$ converge in the limit to stable absolute values, implying stable mass. In other words, only if the growth rate is equal to zero will a physical system of this sort not contradict the conservation of mass condition.

Since the system described here is not protected by the assumption of free gifts that characterizes models of the Neumann type, the conservation of mass condition requires that the dominant eigenvalues of the output matrix be equal to unity. The balanced or steady state (positive) growth rate derived as an equilibrium condition in the major multisector growth models is formally analogous to the limiting growth rate derived for this model. What is important is that in any model a positive equilibrium rate of growth implies the assumption of free gifts. If the free gifts assumption fails, as it must under the conservation of mass condition, then the physical rate of growth of the system, whether on or off a notional equilibrium path, must be zero. In fact, as we will see in the next section of this chapter, the conservation of mass condition contradicts the stationary technology assumption employed to demonstrate this point, but the general result holds trivially, irrespective of the technology employed. If we define the rate of growth of a physical system whether on or off the equilibrium path to be

$$g = [\mathbf{q}(k - 1)\mathbf{e}/\mathbf{q}(k)] - 1 \qquad\qquad 2.16$$

it follows directly from 2.4 that only the zero rate will be admissible.

Although I am not yet concerned with the interactions of economy and environment, it is worth remarking that it is the absurdity of the idea that any one subsystem may expand indefinitely in a finite world that has lead economists to postulate logistic in preference to the exponential growth curves ground out by such models (cf. van Duijn, 1983). Logistic curves have the property that they asymptotically approach a maximum value, suggesting that the economy will attain a stable high plateau in an entirely self-regulating way. But there is no reason at all to suppose that any technologically stationary system will naturally grow in this fashion where it is unconstrained by its environment. Indeed, the natural pattern of growth of biological systems unconstrained by their environment is exponential (Lotka, 1956). That it may be possible to fit a logistic curve to the time path of systems that do run up against environmental constraints indicates only the extent to which the environment is capable of distorting the natural growth paths of constrained systems. There is little empirical foundation for the assumption of a logistic expansion path for any system in the absence of environmental constraints.

2.4   The conservation of mass and the "free disposal" of waste

Consider now the implications of the conservation of mass condition for the utilization of resources and the technology of the system. On the output side we have seen that the conservation of mass condition implies that a closed physical system has a zero growth rate, and that although any subsystem within a closed physical system may be able to expand, it will not be able to expand without limit. Sooner or later it will be bound by the conservation of mass condition. This says nothing, though, about the allocation of resources between processes in a closed system, and the implications of change in the relative quantities of resources available to the system.

The conservation of mass has one very clear implication for the matrix describing the allocation of resources. In a closed physical system, $A(k)$ will fully account for all resources in the system in the kth period. This has already been rather loosely alluded to as a full employment condition. It implies that

$$q(k) = q(k)A(k) \qquad\qquad 2.17$$

for all $k \geq 0$. This follows from the fact that in a closed system there is no free disposal of resources. Waste material cannot be ejected from the system. Consequently, every resource must go somewhere. It should be emphasized, however, that this is not full employment in the usual sense of the term. It does not imply that every economically valued resource should be fully employed in economic activities. It implies only that all resources will effectively be allocated to some process, whether controlled by an economic agent or not, in every period.

To see the difference between this condition and the free disposal case, notice that if the system is protected by the assumption of free disposal, then the condition 2.17 is replaced by the viability condition

$$q(k) \geq q(k)A(k) \qquad\qquad 2.18$$

for all $k \geq 0$. This condition admits the possibility that there will be resources generated within the system that will be unused by the system. In other words, it admits the possibility of unemployment. But it excludes the possibility that resources are used that are not available to the system. It is a weak application of the dictum that nothing can be produced out of nothing. It assumes that resources that are not used may be costlessly dumped either inside or outside the global system.

The significance of 2.17 lies in its implications for the time variability of the system, and so for the general concept of the technologically stationary system. These implications can be drawn out directly by a transparent line of reasoning. The quantity of resources available to the system at the beginning of the kth period is given by $\mathbf{q}(k)$, but the quantity of resources required by the system in terms of the technology inherited from the previous period is given by $\mathbf{q}(k)\mathbf{A}(k-1)$. If there is full employment of all resources under this technology, that is, if $\mathbf{q}(k) = \mathbf{q}(k)\mathbf{A}(k-1)$, then the inherited technology will obviously satisfy the conservation of mass condition 2.17. But if there is less than full employment of all resources or if there is unfulfilled excess demand for any resource, that is, if $\mathbf{q}(k) \neq \mathbf{q}(k)\mathbf{A}(k-1)$, then the inherited technology will not satisfy the conservation of mass condition.

It follows that a jointly determined economy-environment system satisfying the conservation of mass condition may be technologically stationary (implying no change in the level and combination of inputs employed in all processes) only if there is full employment of all resources in all periods. Since, by the conservation of mass condition, $\mathbf{q}(k) = \mathbf{q}(k)\mathbf{A}(k)$ for all $k \geq 0$, $\mathbf{q}(k) \neq \mathbf{q}(k)\mathbf{A}(k-1)$ implies that $\mathbf{A}(k) \neq \mathbf{A}(k-1)$. Hence, $\mathbf{A}(k) = \mathbf{A}(k-1)$ only if the vector of residuals

$$\mathbf{q}_R(k) = \mathbf{q}(k)[\mathbf{I} - \mathbf{A}(k-1)] \qquad 2.19$$

is equal to zero. The assumption that the system is technologically stationary is consistent with the assumption that it is thermodynamically closed only if the system generates no residuals in any period. Moreover, we know from 2.4 that $\underline{\mathbf{a}}_i(k)\mathbf{e} = \underline{\mathbf{b}}_i(k)\mathbf{e}$ for all $i \in \{1, \ldots, n\}$; hence, whenever $\underline{\mathbf{a}}_i(k)\mathbf{e} \neq \underline{\mathbf{a}}_i(k-1)\mathbf{e}$, then $b_{ij}(k) \neq b_{ij}(k-1)$ for at least one $j \in \{1, \ldots, n\}$. In other words, the conservation of mass condition 2.4 insists that any change in the mass of all or any of the inputs to the ith process will be matched by an equivalent change in the mass of any or all outputs of the process.

Consider, however, the case where there is free disposal of residuals in the short period, and the system is bound only by the viability condition 2.18. This case is interesting not because it is held to be a reasonable approximation of the global system, but because it is relevant to the short-period behavior of any subsystem within the global system. In this case the system will be compelled to adapt only if $\mathbf{q}(k) < \mathbf{q}(k)\mathbf{A}(k-1)$, the mass of inputs required for the full utilization of all resources exceeding the mass of resources available. Notice, though, that the adaptation of the system does not necessarily imply technological change. Since the existence of residuals causes no difficulty, it is possible for the system to adapt either by modifying the elements of $\mathbf{A}(k-1)$, or by reducing the quantities of resources advanced in production, implying the scaling of the $q_i(k)$. In other words, if the system is protected by the free disposal assumption, then a binding viability constraint may be relieved either by technological change or by limiting the level of capacity utilization.

The option of regulating the level of capacity utilization should be intuitively obvious, but, to see this, suppose that there exists excess demand for the ith resource in the kth period implying that

$$q_i(k) < \mathbf{q}(k)\mathbf{a}_i(k-1) \qquad\qquad 2.20$$

The quantity of the ith resource available at the beginning of the kth period is less than the quantity of that resource required under the technology inherited from the $k-1$th period. There exists a scalar $\rho < 1$ such that

$$q_i(k) = \mathbf{q}(k)\rho\mathbf{a}_i(k-1) \qquad\qquad 2.21$$

By operating the process or processes using the ith resource of ρ of capacity, the viability condition may be satisfied.

To repeat, the importance of the distinction between conditions 2.17 and 2.18 is that while a closed physical system will always be bound by 2.17, an open system or a subsystem within the (indecomposable) global system may, at any given point in time, be bound only by 2.18. Hence, while any general physical system subject to change in the relative mass of resources will be time varying, it may be possible for distinct subsystems to resist internal change for finite periods by operating below capacity. Indeed, this has historically been the preferred strategy for a number of human economies (Perrings, 1985).

In the general case, however, the time path of the resources of the technologically nonstationary system will not be defined by 2.7, but by

$$\mathbf{q}(k) = \mathbf{q}(0)\prod_i \mathbf{B}(i) \qquad i = 0,1,\ldots,k-1 \qquad\qquad 2.22$$

This is valid whether change is purposive or nonpurposive. The conservation of mass condition forces an adjustment on the system wherever any resources are in excess supply or demand under the inherited technology. This is to say nothing about the direction of such adjustments – whether they are incremental or catastrophic – it is to say only that there will have to be some adjustment. The global system generating residuals does not have the option of standing still, a point we will return to in connection with the stationary state.

CHAPTER 3

Structure and time in the physical system

3.1 The significance of system structure

We have seen that technological change results wherever residuals are generated in the processes of system production subject to the conservation of mass. On the other hand, we know that particular economic systems – and some ecological systems – have changed comparatively little over extended periods. The imperative to change is obviously much weaker at the micro than the macro level. Why? I now consider the implications of system structure both for the pressures to change in technologically stationary or time-invariant subsystems and for the legitimacy of the classical free disposal and free gifts assumptions.

By *assumption 2* the global physical system is indecomposable over its history, implying that it cannot be broken down into historically disjoint subsystems. It is not possible to identify any set of processes that is entirely independent of all other past or present processes. Yet we do commonly assume that it is legitimate to treat particular sets of activities "as if" they were independent. The concept of "final" demand in multisectoral planning models of the Leontief type, for example, supposes that the consumption activities generating such final demands have no feedback effects on the conditions of production of consumer goods. Although the indecomposability assumption asserts that such suppositions are illusory, this chapter considers the conditions in which subsystems of an indecomposable general system may be thought to approximate decomposable systems. In other words, it considers the necessary conditions for discounting the indecomposability of the system.

The decomposability of the pair $\mathbf{A}(k)$, $\mathbf{B}(k)$ implies that it is possible, by permutation of indices, to bring them to the form

$$\mathbf{A}(k) = \begin{bmatrix} \mathbf{A}_{11} & \mathbf{A}_{12} \\ \mathbf{0} & \mathbf{A}_{22} \end{bmatrix} (k) \qquad \mathbf{B}(k) = \begin{bmatrix} \mathbf{B}_{11} & \mathbf{B}_{12} \\ \mathbf{0} & \mathbf{B}_{22} \end{bmatrix} (k) \qquad 3.1$$

If it is not possible to bring both of them to this form, the system is said to be indecomposable. The indecomposability of the system implies that it is not possible to identify a subset of processes, $A_{22}(k)$ and $B_{22}(k)$ in 3.1, that is entirely independent of the rest. It means that every process depends directly or indirectly on every other or, more precisely, that every process directly or indirectly employs the output of every other process.

The indecomposability assumption admits three possibilities:

1. The system is input indecomposable but output decomposable. $A(k)$ is indecomposable but $B(k)$ is decomposable.
2. The system is input decomposable but output indecomposable. $A(k)$ is decomposable but $B(k)$ is indecomposable.
3. The system is both input and output indecomposable. $A(k)$ and $B(k)$ are both indecomposable.

All three possibilities are, however, subject to the restriction that both $A(k)^h$ and $B(k)^h$ are indecomposable for any $h \geq 1$ and for all $k > 0$. If $A(k)^h$ and $B(k)^h$ are decomposable for some $h \geq 1$ and for at least one $k > 0$, it is possible to identify one or more historically independent subsystems within the general system, which contradicts *assumption 2*.

The effect of this restriction is to exclude one important class of indecomposable matrices, the imprimitive or cyclic matrices. An input matrix, $A(k)$, is said to be primitive if it is not possible to bring it, by permutation of the rows and columns, to the form

$$A(k) = \begin{bmatrix} 0 & A_{12} & 0 & \cdots & 0 \\ 0 & 0 & A_{23} & \cdots & 0 \\ \cdots\cdots\cdots\cdots\cdots\cdots\cdots \\ 0 & 0 & 0 & \cdots & A_{n-1\,n} \\ A_{n1} & 0 & 0 & \cdots & 0 \end{bmatrix} (k) \qquad 3.2$$

if we assume simple production, a cyclic or imprimitive input matrix means that the system can be divided into a number of subsystems, each of which produces the inputs required by the next. If there are h such subsystems, this means that the outputs of any one subsystem are converted into its own inputs exactly h periods later. Hence, although $A(k)$ may be indecomposable at any moment in time, if we consider the h periods together, it behaves as if it were a decomposable system.

More particularly, if A is an imprimitive matrix, and if the index of imprimitivity – denoting the number of eigenvalues of equal modulus – is h, then $A^h = \text{diag}[A_1, \cdots, A_n]$. A^h is a block diagonal matrix, with each block having the same dominant eigenvalue (Gantmacher, 1959, pp. 97–98). Considered over the interval $[0, h]$ the system is totally decomposable. It is worth adding that a time-invariant imprimitive system of the form given in 2.7 has the property that the sequence $\{\mathbf{q}(k)\}$ is not convergent, but oscillates around the rate of growth given by the dominant eigenvalue of $\mathbf{B}(k)$. Moreover, the oscillations are undamped (Morishima, 1964, pp. 171–174).

Notice that the indecomposability of $\mathbf{A}(k)$ or $\mathbf{B}(k)$ does not imply anything about the relative sparseness of those matrices. In other words, it does not imply anything about the directness or indirectness of the links between the processes of the system. The relative sparseness of the technology matrices is of interest in that it provides an index of the importance of time in the technical relations between distinct processes. It determines the lag structure of the system.

If $\mathbf{A}(k)$ is strictly positive for all k, implying that each process employs some of every resource available to the system in all periods, then a qualitative or quantitative change in any one resource will have immediate effects on every process in the system. There will be no lags greater than one period. Consider, however, the relatively sparse input matrix:

$$
\mathbf{A}(k) = \begin{bmatrix}
A_{11} & A_{12} & 0 & 0 & 0 & 0 & 0 & 0 \\
0 & A_{22} & A_{23} & 0 & 0 & 0 & 0 & 0 \\
0 & 0 & A_{33} & A_{34} & A_{35} & 0 & 0 & 0 \\
0 & 0 & 0 & A_{44} & 0 & A_{46} & 0 & 0 \\
0 & 0 & 0 & 0 & 0 & A_{56} & A_{57} & 0 \\
0 & 0 & 0 & 0 & 0 & A_{66} & A_{67} & 0 \\
0 & 0 & 0 & 0 & 0 & 0 & A_{77} & A_{78} \\
A_{81} & 0 & 0 & 0 & 0 & 0 & 0 & A_{88}
\end{bmatrix} (k) \qquad 3.3
$$

Let us assume, for expository purposes, that there is simple production. The matrix shown in 3.3 then indicates that the outputs of the processes described by the row of submatrices $\underline{A}_l(k)$, are transformed into the inputs of the processes described by the row $\underline{A}_2(k)$, via a chain $\{\underline{A}_1\} \rightarrow \{\underline{A}_8\} \rightarrow \{\underline{A}_7\} \rightarrow \{\underline{A}_6\} \rightarrow \{\underline{A}_4\} \rightarrow \{\underline{A}_3\} \rightarrow \{\underline{A}_2\}$ involving a seven-period lag.

The sparseness of the technology matrices indicates what may be called the *time distance* between processes. It is the existence of a significant time distance between processes that provides the only possible rationale for the treatment of distinct subsystems "as if" they were independent. In other words, the sparseness of the technology matrices enables one to identify what may be thought of as temporarily independent subsystems within the global system. Because this sparseness builds in a technologically determined delay in the transmission of certain effects around the global system, it is possible to exclude such effects from consideration by arbitrary selection of processes, resources, and time horizons.

3.2   Transactions, exactions, and insertions

We will return to the question of the time distance between processes and the crucial importance of the time perspectives of economic agents later. First, to clarify the concept of the dependence between processes, let us isolate the processes described in the fifth and sixth rows and the sixth and seventh columns of 3.3. We thus have

$$\mathbf{A}(k) = \begin{bmatrix} \mathbf{A}_{56} \ \mathbf{A}_{57} \\ \mathbf{A}_{66} \ \mathbf{A}_{67} \end{bmatrix} (k)$$

$\mathbf{A}(k)$ is now an indecomposable notionally independent system. The forward and backward effects on the processes indexed 1,2,3,4,7,8 are ignored by invoking the assumptions of free disposals and free gifts.

If we now assume that $\mathbf{B}(k)$ is of similar form and if the fifth and sixth rows represent processes operated by two different sets of agents, then each set of agents depends on the other for inputs in all periods. The allocation of resources between these processes involves an exchange between the two sets of agents of the subsystem. We may describe such a real exchange as a *transaction,* and note that a necessary condition for a transaction to take place is the mutual dependence of the agents concerned. If there are no gains from trade, there are no grounds for transactions to occur. The definition of a transaction follows.

A *transaction* implies the real exchange of the outputs of distinct processes to the mutual advantage and by the agreement of the agents involved.

Now consider the submatrix comprising the first and second rows and columns only of 3.3. We now have

$$\mathbf{A}(k) = \begin{bmatrix} \mathbf{A}_{11} \ \mathbf{A}_{12} \\ \mathbf{0} \ \ \ \mathbf{A}_{22} \end{bmatrix} (k)$$

which is of the same form as 3.1, a decomposable matrix. Suppose, once again, that the processes of the first and second rows are operated by two different sets of agents, and assume that $\mathbf{A}_{11}(k)$ and $\mathbf{A}_{22}(k)$ are h and $m - h$ square, respectively. If $a_{ih+1}(k) > 0$ for all $i \in \{1, \dots h\}$, the agents operating the first h processes make use of the $h + 1$th resource. By assumption, the $h + 1$th resource is produced only in the $h + 1$th process. Since $a_{h+1}(k) = 0$ for all $i \in \{1, \ldots, h\}$, the agent operating the $h + 1$th process does not obtain anything directly from the agents operating the first h processes in return. Moreover, since $a_{ij}(k) = 0$ for all $i \in \{h + 1, \ldots, m\}$ and for all $j \in \{1, \ldots, h\}$, none of the processes that do supply resources used in the $h + 1$th process use any of the first h resources, and the agent operating the $h + 1$th process obtains nothing indirectly from those operating the first h processes.

The significance of this is that there can be no advantage to the agent operating the $h + 1$th process in offering the $h + 1$th resource for sale to the agents operating the first h resources. Hence, there is no basis for supposing that an exchange or transaction has taken place. The agents operating the last $m - n$ processes must want something from the agents operating the first h processes for any one of the last $m - n$ resources to be offered for exchange. We have to assume, therefore, that $a_{ih+1}(k) > 0$ for all $i \in \{1, \ldots, h\}$ implies either that the agents operating the first h processes seize the $h + 1$th resource by force majeure, which we may call an *exaction,* or that the agent operating the $h + 1$th process disposes of a quantity of the $h + 1$th resource onto the first h processes, which we may call an *insertion.* Either way, it implies an asymmetrical power relationship between the two sets of agents, and each subsystem represents part of the environment of the other. The definition of exactions and insertions follows.

An *exaction* implies the forcible uncompensated acquisition of the outputs of one process by the agent(s) operating another process.

An *insertion* implies the forcible uncompensated imposition of the outputs of one process, by the agent(s) operating that process, on another process.

If resources that appear in the list of inputs to a process are not transacted, then we may infer that they have either been exacted from the environment of the economy or that they have been inserted by that environment. The concept of exaction covers all forms of environmental exploitation: the pillage and plunder of one human society by another, the hunting and killing of one species by another, the gathering of food plants, or the mining of the earth. All involve the securing of resources through the exercise of force. The concept of insertion is similarly broad, covering both the deliberate and accidental pollution associated with waste disposal, and the controlled introduction of resources into subordinate processes.

Notice that if $\mathbf{B}_{(1,2)}(k)$, the submatrix comprising the first two columns of the first two rows of an output matrix of similar form to 3.3, decomposes in the same way as 3.3. This implies that the first h processes produce quantities of all m resources in the subsystem. Hence there exists a basis for transactions between the proprietors of the first h and the last $m - h$ processes. It is worth repeating, though, that the decomposability of the input matrix in a system of *simple* production would be sufficient to preclude the possibility that all inputs are obtained by transaction.

It is, of course, possible that a single process will be subject to both exactions and insertions by the agents operating some other process. From this it follows that the indecomposability of the $A(k)$ matrix is a necessary but not a sufficient condition for transactions to take place. In an indecomposable economy-environment system, it is the system of signals or the information system and not the structure of the technology matrices that distinguishes the economy from its environment.

3.3   Exaction: the depletion of nondurable resources

Wherever the gross input matrix of a subsystem within a joint economy-environment subsystem is decomposable, the production of resources will involve either exactions or insertions. That is, there will be resources listed in the input coefficients of some processes that have either been obtained or implanted by force. In this and the following sections I consider the significance of the decomposability of the system for the free gifts assumption. Since I ignore the problem of insertions, I tacitly retain the free disposals assumption.

I am interested in the properties of decomposable systems, but not of all decomposable systems. Recall that the total decomposability of the matrix $A(k)$ implies that it may be brought to the form

$$A(k) = \begin{bmatrix} A_{11} & 0 & \ldots & 0 \\ 0 & A_{22} & \ldots & 0 \\ \multicolumn{4}{c}{\ldots\ldots\ldots\ldots\ldots} \\ 0 & 0 & \ldots & A_{hh} \end{bmatrix} (k) \qquad 3.4$$

by permutation of indices. The $A_{ii}(k)$, $i = 1, \ldots, h$, are square indecomposable blocks. The meaning of the total decomposability of $A(k)$ in a system of simple production is simply that while all processes described by any one block on the principle diagonal are mutually dependent, each block is totally independent of the next. Hence, each block describes a discrete, self-sufficient system, which is determined independently of any other. This case is of no conceivable interest.

The partial decomposability of $A(k)$ implies that, in all cases, it is possible to bring it to the form described in 3.1. If each of the square blocks on the principle diagonal is itself decomposable, then the system may be brought by further permutation of indices to the form

$$
A(k) = \begin{bmatrix}
\mathbf{A}_{11} & 0 & \cdots & \mathbf{A}_{1g} & \mathbf{A}_{1g+1} & \cdots & \mathbf{A}_{1h-1} & \mathbf{A}_{1h} \\
0 & \mathbf{A}_{22} & \cdots & \mathbf{A}_{2g} & \mathbf{A}_{2g+1} & \cdots & \mathbf{A}_{2h-1} & \mathbf{A}_{2h} \\
0 & 0 & \cdots & \mathbf{A}_{gg} & \mathbf{A}_{gg+1} & \cdots & \mathbf{A}_{gh-1} & \mathbf{A}_{gh} \\
0 & 0 & \cdots & 0 & \mathbf{A}_{g+1g+1} & \cdots & \mathbf{A}_{g+1h-1} & \mathbf{A}_{g+1n} \\
0 & 0 & \cdots & 0 & 0 & \cdots & \mathbf{A}_{h-1h-1} & 0 \\
0 & 0 & \cdots & 0 & 0 & \cdots & 0 & \mathbf{A}_{hh}
\end{bmatrix}(k) \qquad 3.5
$$

where the blocks on the principal diagonal are all indecomposable. In order to give an interpretation to this, the normal form of a decomposable matrix, we can take each of the two polar cases. The first of these is

$$
A(k) = \begin{bmatrix}
\mathbf{A}_{11} & \mathbf{A}_{12} & \cdots & \mathbf{A}_{1hh-1} & \mathbf{A}_{1h} \\
0 & \mathbf{A}_{22} & \cdots & 0 & 0 \\
\cdots & \cdots & \cdots & \cdots & \cdots \\
0 & 0 & \cdots & \mathbf{A}_{h-1h-1} & 0 \\
0 & 0 & \cdots & 0 & \mathbf{A}_{hh}
\end{bmatrix}(k) \qquad 3.6
$$

In this system the processes described by the row of submatrices $\underline{\mathbf{A}}_1(k)$ make use of the full range of resources produced in the system, but the processes described by the submatrices $\mathbf{A}_{ii}(k)$, $i = 2, \ldots, h$, make no reciprocal claims. Since we have eliminated, by assumption, the possibility of insertions, this means that the processes described in the first row of submatrices are based on the exaction of resources from a number of discrete, completely self-contained, subsystems, the $\mathbf{A}_{ii}(k)$ referred to above. Under the assumption of simple production, each of these produces all it requires: it obtains nothing from any other subsystem. We may think of this as the case in which a single human economy obtains resources from a number of independent environments.

The second polar case is

$$
A(k) = \begin{bmatrix}
\mathbf{A}_{11} & \mathbf{A}_{12} & \cdots & 0 & \mathbf{A}_{1h} \\
0 & \mathbf{A}_{22} & \cdots & 0 & \mathbf{A}_{2h} \\
\cdots & \cdots & \cdots & \cdots & \cdots \\
0 & 0 & \cdots & \mathbf{A}_{h-1h-1} & \mathbf{A}_{h-1h} \\
0 & 0 & \cdots & 0 & \mathbf{A}_{hh}
\end{bmatrix}(k) \qquad 3.7
$$

In this case the processes described by the first $h - 1$ rows of submatrices all make use of the resources produced in the processes described by $A_{hh}(k)$. As before, these latter processes are completely independent of the rest. Each of the subsystems described by the first $h - 1$ isolated blocks on the principal diagonal is independent of the others, but all depend upon the subsystem described by the hth block on the diagonal. We may think of this case as one in which $h - 1$ human economies exist with each exploiting a common environment.

Consider, now, the dynamic problem in such systems. Recall that under any given technology the time path of the vector of resources in the system is given by the difference equation 2.6. Since we are concerned with the exploitation of nondurable resources, $B(k)$ is block diagonal for all $k > 0$. That is,

$$B(k) = \begin{bmatrix} B_{11} & 0 & \cdots & 0 \\ 0 & B_{22} & \cdots & 0 \\ \multicolumn{4}{c}{\dotfill} \\ 0 & 0 & \cdots & B_{hh} \end{bmatrix} (k) \qquad 3.8$$

Notice that the distinction between durable and nondurable resources is separate from the conventional distinction between renewable and exhaustible resources. We are used to thinking of renewable resources as those capable of regeneration over a few decades, and of exhaustible resources as those requiring millennia to regenerate (Fisher, 1981, p. 11). Timber is renewable by such a criterion, oil is not. We cannot, however, say a priori whether timber or oil is the more durable in production since this depends on the way in which each is used. The assumption of this section that we are dealing with nondurable resources does, however, spotlight the importance of the rate of regeneration of resources.

Because we are concerned with nondurable resources, the time path for each subset of resources, if unconstrained by the viability condition, is determined independently of the rest. For each subset of resources at each technology, the general solution to the difference equations of the physical system is of the form

$$q_i(k) = q_i(0)B_{ii}(0)^k \qquad 3.9$$

with $i = 1, \ldots, h$. Under the protective assumptions of free disposals, each subsystem that is not constrained by the viability condition is free to expand at its maximum potential rate.

The free disposals assumption means that the system is subject to the weak viability condition 2.18. This ensures that the quantity of each resource required under the prevailing technology does not exceed the quantity of the resource available to the system. Consequently, in the absence of technological change, the time path of the vector of resources in a subsystem that is constrained by this condition will reflect the necessity to adjust the level of capacity utilization in all processes to one that is sustainable in terms of the productive potential of the processes of its environment. This parallels the now familiar Golden Rule for the maximum sustainable rate of exploitation of a renewable resource (see Dasgupta and Heal, 1979), and points to one of the recurrent themes both of this essay and of environmental literature generally.

A sufficient condition for a time-invariant system characterized by an input matrix of the form 3.6 to be bound by the viability condition at some point in its history is that the potential rate of growth of any one of the environmental subsystems subject to exactions is less than the potential rate of growth of the subsystem making exactions. Under such circumstances the latter will eventually run up against the limits imposed by the environment and will be forced to adjust either the technology of the dependent subsystem or its level of capacity utilization. This very simple and intuitively obvious point is what lies behind the arguments of both advocates and critics of the "pessimistic" models of economy-environment interactions from Malthus to the Club of Rome.

More formally, since the quantity vector corresponding to any time-invariant subsystem unconstrained by the viability condition will converge to a left eigenvector of that system, the own-rate of growth of each resource generated in the ith subsystem will converge to a value equal to $\lambda_{\max}[\mathbf{B}_{ii}(k)] - 1$, where $\lambda_{\max}[\mathbf{B}_{ii}(k)]$ is the dominant eigenvalue of the submatrix $\mathbf{B}_{ii}(k)$. If, in a system in which $\mathbf{A}(k)$ is of the form in 3.6 for all k, $\lambda_{\max}[\mathbf{B}_{11}(k)] > \lambda_{\max}[\mathbf{B}_{ii}(k)]$, then as k tends to infinity

$$\mathbf{q}_i(k) < \mathbf{q}(k)\mathbf{A}_i(k-1) \qquad\qquad 3.10$$

where $\mathbf{A}_i(k-1)$ denotes the ith column of submatrices. There will be unsatisfied excess demand for all resources produced in the ith environmental subsystem. This follows directly from the fact that the right-hand side of 3.10 comprises the sum of $\mathbf{q}_i(k)\mathbf{A}_{ii}(k-1)$, the ith environmental or independent subsystem's requirements of its own resources under the inherited technology, and $\mathbf{q}_1(k)\mathbf{A}_{1i}(k)$, the requirements of the dependent subsystem.

The following strict definition of the renewability and exhaustibility of resources follows naturally. Resources deriving from an independent subsystem subject to exactions may be said to be *renewable* under a given technology if the maximum potential own-rate of growth of the independent subsystem is greater than or equal to that of the dependent subsystem, and may be said to be *exhaustible* if the maximum potential own-rate of growth of the independent subsystem is less than that of the dependent subsystem. More precisely, resources yielded by the processes having outputs $\mathbf{B}_{ii}(k)$ in 3.8, $i = 2, \ldots, h$, may be defined as being renewable if $\lambda_{max}[\mathbf{B}_{11}(k)] \leq \lambda_{max}[\mathbf{B}_{ii}(k)]$, and may be defined as exhaustible if $\lambda_{max}[\mathbf{B}_{11}(k)] > \lambda_{max}[\mathbf{B}_{ii}(k)]$.

Notice, though, that the time taken for the general system to converge on the limits imposed by the ith independent subsystem depends both on the difference in growth potential of the dependent and independent subsystems, $\lambda_{max}[\mathbf{B}_{11}(k)]/\lambda_{max}[\mathbf{B}_{ii}(k)]$, and on the difference in the mass of the resources initially available to each, $\mathbf{q}_1(0)\mathbf{e}/\mathbf{q}_i(0)\mathbf{e}$. The larger the mass of resources in the independent relative to the dependent subsystem, the longer will be the time taken for the general system to converge on the limits imposed by the viability constraint. Resources in sufficiently large initial supply to ensure that they will not constrain the growth of any dependent subsystem over the specified time horizon are defined to be physically nonscarce. An economic definition of scarcity will be offered in Chapter 5.

The difference between the two polar cases of production by exaction is that in the case described by 3.6, the dependent subsystem described by row $\underline{\mathbf{A}}_1(k)$ is potentially limited by each of the discrete independent subsystems described by the last $h - 1$ isolated blocks on the principal diagonal, whereas in the case described by 3.7 each of the discrete dependent subsystems described by the first $h - 1$ isolated blocks on the principal diagonal is potentially limited by the independent subsystem described by $\mathbf{A}_{hh}(k)$.

The importance of the second case is that the time taken for the convergence of each of the dependent subsystems on the limits imposed by the common environment is a function of the rate at which all others are making exactions on that environment, as well as the difference in growth potential and initial size of the stock of resources between the dependent and independent subsystems. In other words, the second case is one in which the environment of each dependent subsystem includes a number of such subsystems, each of which competes for the same resources. In a physical sense this opens up the problem of the common discussed in later chapters.

One final point to make about systems of production by exaction of nondurable resources is that the condition for the environment not to limit the system, at least potentially, is that the dominant eigenvalue of each block on the principal diagonal of the matrix $\mathbf{B}(0)$ should be the same. In a system bound by the conservation of mass condition, this would imply not only that each subsystem in the general system had the same potential rate of growth, but also that this potential rate is the zero rate. In other words, it would imply that $\lambda_{max}[\mathbf{B}_{ii}(k)] = 1$ for all $i \in \{1, \ldots, h\}$.

3.4   Exaction: the depletion of durable resources

Consider, now, the problem of production by exaction of durable environmental resources. The meaning of simple production is not just that each product is produced by one process only. It is also that all materials used in the production of that one product depreciate completely in each period. Once we admit the possibility that resources exacted from the environment of any referent system (including any human economy) may not depreciate completely in each period, then the dynamics of the system change. If the resources exacted from the several environmental subsystems described in 3.6 are durable, then it follows that the corresponding net output matrix will not be diagonal, but will be of the same form as $\mathbf{A}(k)$. That is,

$$\mathbf{B}(k) = \begin{bmatrix} \mathbf{B}_{11} & \mathbf{B}_{12} & \cdots & \mathbf{B}_{1hh-1} & \mathbf{B}_{1h} \\ \mathbf{0} & \mathbf{B}_{22} & \cdots & \mathbf{0} & \mathbf{0} \\ \cdots & \cdots & \cdots & \cdots & \cdots \\ \mathbf{0} & \mathbf{0} & \cdots & \mathbf{B}_{h-1h-1} & \mathbf{0} \\ \mathbf{0} & \mathbf{0} & \cdots & \mathbf{0} & \mathbf{B}_{hh} \end{bmatrix}(k) \qquad 3.11$$

In this case, if we assume that $\mathbf{B}(k) = \mathbf{B}(0)$ for all $k \geq 0$, the quantity vector of the system will, if unconstrained by the viability condition, converge to left eigenvector of $\mathbf{B}(k)$ corresponding to $\lambda_{max}[\mathbf{B}(k)]$ only if $\lambda_{max}[\mathbf{B}(k)] = \lambda_{max}[\mathbf{B}_{11}(k)]$, and $\lambda_{max}[\mathbf{B}(k)] > \lambda_{max}[\mathbf{B}_{ii}(k)]$ for all $i \in \{2, \ldots, h\}$. That is, if the system is unconstrained by the viability condition, the quantity vector will converge to a state in which all resources are growing at the same rate if and only if the maximum potential growth rate of the system is the same as the maximum potential growth rate of the processes described by the row $\underline{\mathbf{B}}_1(k)$, the economy in this example.

The reason that the system may converge to a rate of growth greater than the rate of growth of the subsystems from which exactions are made, is that if "natural" resources are durable, the undepreciated part of the exacted resources adds to the general stock of such resources available to the economy in each period. Of course, if the system is bound by the conservation of mass condition this implies that the con-

dition for convergence of the structure of production of the economy
is that it have a potential rate of growth of zero.

If the matrix $\mathbf{A}(k)$ is of the form in 3.7, and if the resources exacted
from the processes described by the block $\mathbf{A}_{hh}(k)$ are durable, then $\mathbf{B}(k)$
will be of similar form. In such circumstances the quantity vector will
be convergent only if the maximum potential growth rate of the system
is the same as the maximum potential growth rate of each of the
dependent subsystems making exactions on the common set of
resources, and if this rate is greater than the maximum potential
growth rate of the processes yielding that set of resources. Once again,
however, if the system is bound by the conservation of mass condition,
then it follows that convergence of the quantity vector supposes that
the maximum potential growth rate of each of the dependent subsystems, the set of discrete economies in this example, is the zero rate.

Whether resources are durable or not, any system of production by
exaction is ultimately limited by the environment on which it makes
exactions, and the options for a system of production by exaction in
the face of a binding environmental constraint reduce to the regulation
of capacity utilization, or adaptation of the technology informing the
use made of exacted resources, or some combination of the two. However, providing that the time horizon of the agents of the system making the exactions is less than the time taken to run into the viability
constraint, it is possible to treat the subsystem as if environmental
resources are the free gifts of nature. Thus, in a static economy-environment model where the viability constraint is not currently binding,
the assumption of free gifts is logically tenable, though of little real
interest.

3.5   Insertion: durable and nondurable residuals

In order to discuss the limits of production by exaction I have so far
made the convenient but fictional assumption of the free disposal of
residuals. The pollution problem exists because, as Boulding reminded
us over twenty years ago (1966), the assumption of free disposal does
not hold in a materially closed system. What is more, the assumption
of free disposal hides a difficulty as great or greater than the difficulty
associated with the assumption of free gifts. Indeed, the thrust of much
of the work on the economics of the environment during the last fif-
teen years has been that whereas the human economy was in the past
most constrained by the limited availability of natural resources, it is
currently most constrained by the pollution associated with the disposal of wastes. So, for example, Daly has argued that whereas "the

classical economists thought that the steady state would be made necessary by limits on the depletion side (the law of increasing cost or diminishing returns) . . . the main limits in fact seem to be occurring on the pollution side" (1973, p. 17).

In part, this derives from the sheer enormity of the waste problem. Ayres and Kneese (1969), in arguing the importance of the conservation of mass principle, made the point graphically, if not entirely correctly. The mass of all resources extracted from the environment was, they maintained, exactly equal to the mass of all wastes returned to the environment. Although, as Victor (1972) has subsequently pointed out, this misleadingly defined accumulation as waste, it did give some sense of the increase in the quantities of waste products being imposed on the environment. Whether or not recorded increases in real output were exactly matched by increases in waste disposal, the notion that the one closely tracks the other made it easy to see that the other side of an aggressive drive for growth in material output is a reckless attitude to the waste burden. The environment has been required to accommodate an enormous and growing mass of waste products. This has been compounded by a change in the nature of such products. The conversion of nondurable, nontoxic raw materials into highly durable, highly toxic waste products is as much a characteristic of modern production processes as is the increasing mass of wastes.

The problem at issue here is the significance of system structure for the effects of insertions or residuals disposals into the environment. In this section I assume that, consistent with the conservation of mass, $q(k) = q(k)A(k)$ for all $k \geq 0$. The allocation matrix fully accounts for all resources in all periods. The effect of a change in the nature or level of the residuals generated within the economy and disposed of within the environment of that economy depends, once again, on the structure of the allocation matrix.

It was argued in Chapter 2 that a closed system subject to the law of the conservation of mass might be technologically stationary only if it generated no residuals in any period. The problem now is whether a subset of processes comprising the economy in a joint, materially closed, economy-environment system may be technologically stationary despite the generation of residuals. Implicit in the notion of free disposals in a technologically stationary system is the idea that waste resources may be allocated in such a way that they will have no effect on either the processes yielding the waste products or on the environment that provides the raw materials for those processes. If waste products generated within the processes of a human economy are to have no effect on those processes, they must be disposed of in environments that have no direct or indirect connection with the economy. It is easy to see that this will only be true if the input matrix in a system of simple production is decomposable.

Consider, again, the formal form of the decomposable matrix $A(k)$ in 3.5, and suppose that the economy is described by the rows $\underline{A}_g(k)$ and $\underline{A}_{g+1}(k)$. The environmental processes from which the economy obtains its raw materials are then described by the rows $\underline{A}_i(k)$, $i = g + 2, \ldots, h$; and the environmental processes into which the economy inserts its waste products are described by the rows $\underline{A}_j(k)$, $j = 1, \ldots, g - 1$. The economy is thus in a position of dominance over two distinct sets of environmental processes: one its source of raw materials, its environmental larder, the other the receptacle into which it pours its wastes, its environmental sink. In such a case the economy is fully protected from the effects of the disposal of wastes so long as the processes of its environmental sink do not feed into the processes of its environmental larder.

Since the gross input matrix of the general system is not decomposable, it will only be possible to model the system as if decomposable if the time distance between the processes of the environmental larder and the environmental sink exceeds the arbitrary time horizon of the agents of the system. In other words, an indecomposable but sparse input matrix may be seen as decomposable by those with reason to be myopic.

Of course, in the real world the time distance between processes is unlikely to be known, for reasons to be explored in later chapters. Historically, the disposal of wastes in the environment of the human economy has often been made in ignorance of the relations of technical dependence in the system. The links between the processes of the environment have been relatively opaque. Thus, even though the disposal of residuals in the environment has subsequently proved to have an impact on the processes of the economy, the necessity for such an impact has not been apparent at the time the disposals were made. Of the many reasons for the failure to see the connections between the processes of the environment in the real world, one is undoubtedly the length of the chain connecting the various processes on which the economy depends.

Take the relatively sparse input matrix, 3.3. If we suppose that the processes of the economy are recorded in rows 7 and 8, and that positive entries in $A_{78}(k)$ represent insertions into the environment, while positive entries in $A_{81}(k)$ represent exactions on the environment, then it is easy to see that a quantitative or qualitative change in the outputs of the processes described by the row of submatrices $\underline{A}_7(k)$, will affect the processes described by the row $\mathbf{A_8}(k)$, but only via the chain $\{\mathbf{A_6}\}$ → $\{\mathbf{A_4}\}$ → $\{\mathbf{A_3}\}$ → $\{\mathbf{A_2}\}$ → $\{\mathbf{A_1}\}$ → $\{\mathbf{A_8}\}$. The longer the chain, the longer the delay in the effects of any given change.

Whether or not it is "rational" for the agents of the economy to take account of the delayed effects of any pollution of the environment will depend on whether their time horizon is less than the time distance between the processes $\{\mathbf{A_4}\}$ and $\{\mathbf{A_5}\}$ – the length of the delay before the effects of any disposal emerge. Whether or not significant delayed effects will exist will depend on the various properties of the pollutants, such as their toxicity and their durability. It is, for example, the durability of certain toxic metals that ensures their effectiveness over a long and complex food chain. Moreover, the timing and nature of the effects of pollution will depend on whether the directly affected processes merely transmit the pollutants or are themselves altered. All that can be said at a general level is that a necessary condition for pollution to have some effect on a particular process is that a chain exists between the polluting and polluted processes.

Disposals may affect both the level and composition of the outputs of the processes of the environment. Any disposals affecting the level of outputs of the environment will affect both the absolute limits on the expansion of the system imposed by the environment and the time taken for the system to converge on those limits. This last point is crucial to an understanding of the physical basis of fluctuations and the bunching of innovations. For now it is sufficient to note that if the own-rate of physical surplus of a process subject to exactions increases (decreases) as a result of the disposal of residuals in the environment, and if that process potentially limits the system, then the time taken for the system to run up against the limits imposed by the process will be lengthened (shortened). So an action that causes, say, the erosion of arable land, will result in a reduction in the quantity of such land available and bring forward the point at which land scarcity begins to constrain the system. On the other hand, disposals that affect the composition of outputs of the processes of the environment, either by distortion of those outputs or by the addition of durable compounds, will affect the composition of the resources exacted from the environment by the processes of the economy. The insertion of suspended particulates or compounds of nitrogen and sulphur in the air will, for example, result in a qualitative change in an output of the environment that is basic to all human production processes.

In conclusion, it is worth repeating that whether we are considering a problem of exaction or insertion, depletion or pollution, any subsystem operating within an indecomposable physical system will be limited by the effects of its actions on its environment. In a general sense, no one process can be thought to be independent of the rest. But for any sparse system, the time taken for the effects of different actions to flow through the system provides a subjective rationale for the myopic decomposition of the system and all the major economic models of depletion and pollution involve such a decomposition. The rates of time preference that underpin such myopic vision are accordingly a crucial factor in the way we perceive our dependence on the processes of the environment.

CHAPTER 4

Technological change and the environmental constraints to physical growth

4.1 "The limits to growth"

No matter how sparse the technology matrices, no matter how tenuous the connections between the various productive processes that make up the global system, an increase in the level of activity of any one subsystem will eventually have repercussions on the environment of that subsystem. The conservation of mass condition ensures both that no one subsystem can expand indefinitely and that the more any subsystem expands, the more the whole system must change.

The meaning of the environmental limits to growth, and the role of technological change in removing those limits, was debated in the extraordinarily heated exchanges over the Club of Rome report (Meadows et al., 1972). The report, using results generated by the so-called "Doomsday Models" developed by Forrester (1971), condemned the allegedly reckless growth orientation of the economics profession. This excited economists to launch a series of more or less damning counterattacks. Vituperative individual indictments of the model, by such as Beckerman (1972), were complemented by the more measured but sustained indictments of various symposia (see *Review of Economic Studies,* 1974; Weintraub et al., 1973).

The issues were apparently quite simple. The Forrester models showed that in a finite world where, by implicit assumption, the elasticity of substitution in global production was either very low or zero, the exponential growth of any one subsystem inevitably ran it up against the limits imposed by the availability of basic resources. On the other side, it was argued that in a finite world where, by explicit assumption, the elasticity of substitution in global production was very high, the rising scarcity of natural resources subject to exponentially increasing rates of exploitation by any one subsystem would induce substitution into less scarce resources – with no necessary check on the rate of growth of the subsystem concerned.

Though no economists seem to have objected to the logic of the proposition that the growth of technologically stationary systems in the face of an exhaustible supply of resources would be limited, almost all of them thought it to be an uninteresting and irrelevant proposition (see, for example, Solow, 1973). The notion that human economies would be blindly driven to destruction, without anyone reading the signs along the way, seemed somewhat fanciful. More particularly, economists could not believe that the price signals could be so wrong that nothing would be done to avert the crisis caused by the complete exhaustion of a basic set of resources. As Beckerman put it, "for a team that makes such a fuss about its discovery of 'feed-backs,' they give precious little attention to the economic negative feed-backs that would upset their whole system. By this I mean the incentives to new exploration, recycling, and the use of substitutes that would be occurring gradually as the increasing scarcity of any product led to an upwards trend in its price" (1972, pp. 337–388).

Anyone reconsidering the significance of economy-environment interactions does so in the shadow of this unfortunate debate, and the knowledge that Beckerman's complacent dismissal of *The Limits to Growth* as an "impudent piece of nonsense" is now the received view. This is a problem, not because *The Limits to Growth* was right – except in terms of its very particular assumptions – but because it has crowded out every question of dynamic significance raised by the Doomsday Models. The problems of optimal resource depletion and pollution have been reduced to the same essentially static allocative problem addressed in the timeless Walrasian exchange models. In particular, the long-run implications of complementarity among categories of input and the possibility of unpleasant surprises have simply been ruled out of court. Instead, we have well-rehearsed declarations of belief in the standard assumptions of the Walrasian model, and a touching faith in the serendipitous nature of all things unexpected. Feige and Blau (1980) are typical: "It is our view that the application of neoclassical economic theory to the natural resource area provides a much more powerful and illuminating framework for considering these issues and allows consideration of factors that will be powerful determinants of future resource use but which have been consistently underestimated by the forecasts of doom throughout the years. The most significant of these factors are surely the extraordinary substitution possibilities (in both consumption and production) induced by changes in the relative prices of resources and the often unpredictable and dramatic technological innovations which provide alternative means of satisfying human needs" (1980, p. 110).

On the question of depletion, the inference is that physical resource scarcity as such has "no obvious economic meaning or necessary economic consequences" (1980, p. 111). The economic problem is one of relative scarcity. As the relative price of minerals rise, mines will go deeper, grades will fall, and recycling will increase. The fact that, as Boulding (1966) reminded us, there is no law of increasing material entropy is taken to mean that the relative scarcity of resources is in fact reversible. Providing that sufficient energy is available, it is theoretically possible to reconstitute every natural resource in industrial use. It waits only on the "right" price to be struck for the perfect recycling of a fully extracted resource.

On the question of pollution, the inference is that, given an adequate measure of the real costs of pollution, there is no technical reason why appropriate pollution controls should not be developed. Fisher (1981), echoing Beckerman, makes it plain that he believes pollution to be reducible to a static misallocation problem. For a given set of relative prices (the price set for a given period) it is possible to determine the optimal measure of pollution control. The controllability of the environment is, by implication, merely a matter of allocating sufficient resources to do the job. Given the right price, pollution may be limited to the socially optimal level.

Detailed consideration of optimal depletion and pollution theory is deferred to Chapter 9. What is important here is the assertion that the Doomsday Models are irrelevant because there is no meaning to be given either to the absolute scarcity of natural resources or to the uncontrollability of environmental conditions. The general questions raised by the Doomsday Models about the sustainability of growth in a finite, interdependent, world have been preempted by the assumption that the environmental limits to growth are a function of the resources devoted to environmental control. There are no meaningful absolute limits. The economy – a subsystem within the global system – may apparently expand indefinitely without damage to its environment.

This chapter considers the capacity of controlled technological change to affect the limits imposed by the environment on systems of the type described in the Doomsday Models. The problem is thus the role of controlled technological change in enabling the agents of the human economy to "manage" their environment, so as to extend the life of resources in fixed supply, and to minimize the damaging effects of waste disposal.

4.2   Technological change

Recall that technology, in this essay, means the pool of knowledge that bounds all the material transformations of the general system. It represents the sum of all historically acquired genetic, intuitive, or recorded knowledge of material transformations. Since I assume that the technology matrices of the physical system described above are complete, there is no knowledge existing outside the system that is available to the agents of the system. This does not, of course, mean that there is no knowledge outside the processes undertaken in a given subsystem at a given point in time. The technology applied in the material transformations of any one subsystem in any one period is, by definition, no more than a subset of the technology applied in the material transformations of the general system over all periods in its history. It is therefore useful to make the conventional distinction between technology and technique, where technique refers to the part of the technology available in the general system that is actually applied in the process or processes under consideration. For any one producer, indeed for any one subsystem, there is always a choice of technique.

In terms of the human economy, the distinction between technical and technological change corresponds to the Shumpeterian distinction between innovation and invention. Innovation represents the application of knowledge currently or historically available to the economy. Invention represents controlled technological change: the deliberate application of resources in new combinations or new forms. Hence, innovation refers only to the choice of technique under a given technology, while invention refers to a deliberate qualitative change in that technology. The characterization of invention as controlled technological change distinguishes it from change that follows from the random application of resources in the process of waste disposal since, as we have already seen, technological change in the general sense is a function of residuals disposals – whether planned or unplanned.

From our analysis of the convergence properties of physical systems of the type described here, we know that the convergence of the structure of production [defined by the norm of the quantity vector, $\mathbf{q}(k)$] will occur in a technologically stationary system only if there is free disposal of resources in excess supply. Wherever residuals are disposed of in a closed resource system, the technology of the system will itself change. The necessity for technological change to follow the disposal of residuals in a closed resource system holds whenever $\mathbf{A}(k) \neq \mathbf{I}$. Since, as we have seen, the conservation of mass requires the satisfaction of the equality $\mathbf{q}(k) = \mathbf{q}(k)\mathbf{A}(k)$ for all $k \geq 0$, wherever $q_i(k) < \mathbf{q}(k)\mathbf{a}_i(k-1)$, $i \in \{1, \ldots, n\}$, there will exist a matrix $\mathbf{A}_\Delta (k-1)$ in which there is at least one positive element, such that $\mathbf{q}(k)\mathbf{A}_\Delta (k-1) = \mathbf{q}(k)[\mathbf{I} - \mathbf{A}(k-1)]$. Moreover, from the same conservation of mass condition, $\mathbf{a}_i(k)\mathbf{e} = \mathbf{b}_i(k)\mathbf{e}$ for all i and for all $k \geq 0$. Consequently, if $\mathbf{A}_\Delta (k-1)$ has at least one positive element, then the corresponding change matrix on the output side, $\mathbf{B}_\Delta (k-1)$, will also have at least one positive element.

Notice, though, that the necessity for technological change (in this general sense) tells us only that any closed resource system will adapt to the existence of residuals in some way. It does not tell us how the system will adapt. It does not tell us whether technological change will be controlled (invention) or uncontrolled. All that can be said a priori is that a change in the technology matrices associated with a change in the choice of technique in any one subsystem will not, in general, be sufficient to explain the adaptation of the general system.

To see this, consider a subsystem of the general system described by the rows of submatrices $\underline{\mathbf{A}}_1(k)\underline{\mathbf{B}}_1(k)$ in 4.1:

$$\mathbf{A}(k) = \begin{bmatrix} \mathbf{A}_{11} & \mathbf{A}_{12} \\ \mathbf{A}_{21} & \mathbf{A}_{22} \end{bmatrix}(k) \quad \mathbf{B}(k) = \begin{bmatrix} \mathbf{B}_{11} & 0 \\ 0 & \mathbf{B}_{22} \end{bmatrix}(k) \qquad 4.1$$

where $[\mathbf{A}_{11}\ \mathbf{A}_{12}](k)$ and $[\mathbf{B}_{11}\ 0](k)$ are $m \times n$ matrices, and $[\mathbf{A}_{21}\ \mathbf{A}_{22}](k)$ and $[0\ \mathbf{B}_{22}](k)$ are $(n-m) \times n$. Assume that the agents operating these processes have perfect records. They possess a $k+1$ page catalogue of blueprints, each page detailing the techniques applied in the correspondingly numbered period in the history of the system. Assume that the system is innovative, but not inventive. It admits a choice of recorded techniques for the production of a given set of outputs, but it does not admit the addition of new techniques or new outputs. The pair $\underline{\mathbf{A}}_1(k+1)\ \underline{\mathbf{B}}_1(k+1)$ is then selected from the $m(k+1) \times n$ matrix constructed by recording the techniques applied in every period of the history of the system for the production of each good:

$$\mathbf{A}(k) = \begin{bmatrix} \mathbf{a}_{11}(0) & \cdots & \mathbf{a}_{1n}(0) \\ \cdots & & \cdots \\ \mathbf{a}_{11}(k) & \cdots & \mathbf{a}_{1n}(k) \\ \cdots & & \cdots \\ \mathbf{a}_{m1}(0) & \cdots & \mathbf{a}_{mn}(0) \\ \cdots & & \cdots \\ \mathbf{a}_{m1}(k) & \cdots & \mathbf{a}_{mn}(k) \end{bmatrix}(k)$$

$$\mathbf{B}(k) = \begin{bmatrix} \mathbf{b}_{11}(0) & \cdots & 0 \\ \cdots & & \cdots \\ \mathbf{b}_{11}(k) & \cdots & 0 \\ \cdots & & \cdots \\ 0 & \cdots & \mathbf{b}_{mn}(0) \\ \cdots & & \cdots \\ 0 & \cdots & \mathbf{b}_{mn}(k) \end{bmatrix}(k) \qquad 4.2$$

If only the most efficient n processes are selected to produce the n outputs of the system, then it follows that the system has a choice of a maximum of $(k + 1)^m$ sets of processes. On the assumption that any excess supply will be taken up by the environment (in order to satisfy the conservation of mass conditions 2.4 and 2.5), the system will have to satisfy the weak viability constraint 2.18. This requires that $\mathbf{q}_1(k + 1) \mathbf{A}_{11}(k + 1) \leq \mathbf{q}_1(k + 1)$, $\mathbf{q}_1(k + 1) \mathbf{A}_{12}(k + 1) \leq \mathbf{q}_2(k + 1)$, $\mathbf{q}(k + 1)$ being partitioned conformably with 4.1. The number of combinations of processes satisfying this restriction, a number less than or equal to $(k + 1)^m$, defines the number of feasible sets of processes.

Now if the pair $\underline{\mathbf{A}}_1(k + 1) \underline{\mathbf{B}}_1(k + 1)$ is a subset of processes in an indecomposable system, then $\overline{\mathbf{q}}_1(k + 1) \mathbf{A}_{11}(k + 1)$ and $\mathbf{q}_1(k + 1) \mathbf{A}_{12}(k + 1)$ will be strictly less than $\mathbf{q}_1(k + 1)$ and $\mathbf{q}_2(k + 1)$ respectively – the subsystem will not account for all the resources it uses. More particularly, $\mathbf{q}_1(k + 1) \mathbf{A}_{11}(k + 1) < \mathbf{q}_1(k + 1)$ implies that the subsystem generates residuals that have to enter the processes of the environment. Similarly, $\mathbf{q}_1(k + 1) \mathbf{A}_{12}(k + 1) < \mathbf{q}_2(k + 1)$ implies that environmental resources are being extracted at a positive rate. The first leaves entirely open the question of pollution, the second leaves entirely open the question of depletion. The question of choice of technique has nothing to say about the view that the agents of the human economy may use controlled technological change to relieve the environmental constraints to growth.

4.3   Technological change as a control process

While the theory of control is increasingly being brought to bear on economic problems, the notion that invention in human economies may be conceptualized as a control process is still relatively rare. Other disciplines have long noticed the role of feedback mechanisms in technological change. The early evolution of agricultural technologies, the transition from hunting and gathering to agriculture, for example, has been explained by archeologists in terms of a controlled feedback process (see Bender, 1975). Analogously, the process of evolution by natural selection, the process of acquiring genetic "knowledge," has been convincingly analyzed in very similar terms (see Lotka, 1956; Rendel, 1968). Economists have not, however, looked at the heuristic as opposed to the technical value of control theory.

The important point about planned as opposed to unplanned technological change is that it involves the application of residuals to the system in order to achieve a particular result. It is a process that has all the characteristics of a controlled feedback process: the application of a (linear) combination of the resources, or state variables, of the system to change it from an initial state to some other state. In other words, controlled technological change seeks to change the combination of resources available to the system in future periods by changing the combination of resources advanced now.

The particular advantage of this approach to the description of technological change is that it very clearly establishes the limitations of decisions on the level and combination of inputs in a particular subsystem as means of controlling the general system. It is, for example, a simple matter to establish the conditions that are necessary and sufficient for the general system to be controllable, and the conditions that are necessary and sufficient for partial control to have no feedback effects beyond the controlled process(es).

The mechanical description of technological change as a control process is straightforward. The first-order difference equation that defines the output of the general system in the kth period, $\mathbf{q}(k + 1) = \mathbf{q}(k)\mathbf{B}(k)$, may, as we have seen, be written in the form

$$\mathbf{q}(k + 1) = \mathbf{q}(k)[\mathbf{B}(k - 1) + \mathbf{B}_\Delta (k - 1)] \qquad 4.3$$

where $\mathbf{B}(k - 1)$ represents the technology inherited from the previous period, and $\mathbf{B}_\Delta(k - 1)$ represents the changes brought about in the elements of $\mathbf{B}(k - 1)$ by the planned or unplanned disposal of residuals. If we make, for expository purposes, the very strong assumption that all technological change is controlled, 4.3 may be written in the form of the state-space representation of a linear feedback control system:

$$\mathbf{q}(k + 1) = \mathbf{q}(k)[\mathbf{B}(k - 1) + \mathbf{j}(k)\mathbf{M}(k)] \qquad 4.4$$

In 4.4 $\mathbf{j}(k)$, the n-dimensional row vector of control variables applied at the beginning of the kth period, is a linear combination of the state variables, $\mathbf{q}(k)$; and $\mathbf{M}(k)$ is an n-square feedback matrix describing the changes brought about in the elements of $\mathbf{B}(k - 1)$. The vector of control variables is the vector of residual resources generated by the system in the kth period under the technology inherited from the $k - 1$th period. Hence, we can be more precise about the nature of this feedback matrix. Since

$$\mathbf{j}(k) = \mathbf{q}(k)[\mathbf{I} - \mathbf{A}(k - 1)] \qquad 4.5$$

if $[\mathbf{I} - \mathbf{A}(k - 1)]$ is nonsingular,

$$\mathbf{M}(k) = [\mathbf{I} - \mathbf{A}(k - 1)]^{-1}\mathbf{B}_\Delta(k - 1) \qquad 4.6$$

A nonstationary system of the type described here is said to be controllable if, for any initial state, $\mathbf{q}(0)$, and any final state, $\mathbf{q}(f)$, there exists a finite period, k, and a control sequence, $\{j(t)\}$, $t = 0, \ldots ,$ $k - 1$, such that $q(k) = q(f)$. More generally, such a system may be said to be controllable if it is possible to transform it into a system in which none of the state variables, the $q_i(k)$, are independent of the control vector (cf. Freeman, 1965). What this says is that the structure of the resources produced in the global system may be brought to a particular state in a finite period through the application of residuals to the system only if the production of all resources in the system is determined by the control variables.

Formally, the controllability of such a system implies the $kn \times n$ controllability matrix constructed for an n-dimensional system controlled over k periods, $J(k)$, is of rank n. (First proved by Wonham, 1967. See also Aoki, 1976). To get a feel for the meaning of this notice, first, that the controllability matrix is formed from the sequence of state and feedback matrices as follows:

$$J(k) = \begin{bmatrix} M(0) \\ B(0)M(1) \\ B(1)B(0)M(2) \\ \cdots\cdots\cdots\cdots \\ \prod_t B(t)M(k-1) \end{bmatrix} \qquad t = 0,\ldots,k-2 \qquad 4.7$$

This matrix describes the effects of the controls applied to the system over the k periods of the control sequence. Its importance in the determination of the final state may be seen from the equation giving the general solution of the controlled nonstationary system – called the system transition equation:

$$q(f) = q(0)\prod_t B(t) + \sum_t j(t)[\prod_h B(h)]M(t) \qquad 4.8$$
$$t = 0,\ldots,k-1; h = 0,\ldots,t-1$$

The first term on the right-hand side of 4.8 describes the contribution of the initial stock of resources. The second rather more complicated term describes the contribution of the controls over the interval $[0,k - 1]$. Notice that the second term is in fact the product of the $kn \times n$ controllability matrix $J(k)$ and the kn-dimensional vector, $j(0,k)$, formed by combining the control vectors $j(t)$ over the same interval.

Now it is intuitively obvious that if the structure of all outputs in the system is to be controlled, the vector

$$q(f) - q(0)\prod_t B(t) = j(0,k)J(k) \qquad t = 0,\ldots,k-1 \qquad 4.9$$

will have no zero-valued components. That is, the application of the controls will affect all resources. The matrix $J(k)$ must be of full rank (it cannot have any columns comprising only zeros). In other words, if the system is to be controllable, it must be possible to affect every resource in it. This means that the controlling agency must be able to intervene in the production of every resource. If the feedback matrices describing the technological changes associated with the control are of less than full rank, the controls will not reach all the resources produced in the system.

Symmetrical to the problem of controllability is the problem of observability. The observability of a system implies that it is possible to determine the state of the system by measuring the signals that are its "outputs" in a control sense. Specifically, a system is said to be observable if, for any initial state, $q(0)$, and any final state, $q(f)$, there exists a finite period, k, and a control-output sequence, $\{k(t)\}$, $t = 0$, ...,$k - 1$, such that a knowledge of $\{k(t)\}$ and $q(f)$ is sufficient to determine $q(0)$. The necessary and sufficient conditions for a system to be observable parallel the conditions for its controllability. In particular, a system will be observable if and only if the observability matrix, $K(k)$, formed from the sequence of state and output matrices, is of full rank.

If we define the "control outputs" of the system to be the residuals of that system, then $K(k)$ will have the form

$$K(k) = \begin{bmatrix} [I - A(0)] \\ [I - A(1)]B(0) \\ [I - A(2)]B(1)B(0) \\ \cdots\cdots\cdots\cdots\cdots \\ [I - A(k - 1)]\prod_t B(t) \end{bmatrix} \qquad t = 0, \ldots k - 2 \qquad 4.10$$

The system will be observable if $[I - A(h)]$ is of rank n for all $h \in \{0, \ldots, k - 1\}$. In other words, the system will be observable if the outputs in a control sense are not independent of the state variables.

4.4   The limits of control

The limitations of technological change as a means of controlling the system begin to become apparent when we start to distinguish between the processes of the economy and the processes of the environment, and once we drop the assumption that all residuals are applied to the system in a controlled way. Let the technology matrices be partitioned as in 4.1 to separate the subsystem of the environment from that of the economy, making the assumption that the gross input matrix is indecomposable and that the net output matrix is totally decomposable. In 4.1 let the submatrices A_{11}, A_{12}, and B_{11} describe the inputs and outputs of the first m processes of the system, the processes of the economy, and let the submatrices A_{21}, A_{22}, and B_{22} describe the inputs and outputs of the last $n - m$ processes of the system, the processes of the environment. Let the vector $q(k)$ be partitioned comfortably.

Suppose that the outputs of the system in a control sense are the residuals generated by the economy: that is, the quantity of economic resources in excess supply under the inherited technology of each period. In the tth period they are given by $q_i(t)[I - A_{11}(t - 1)]$. Hence, the $kn \times n$ observability submatrix for a control sequence of k periods is of the form

$$K(k) = \begin{bmatrix} \begin{bmatrix} [I - A_{11}(0)] \,|\, 0 \\ 0 \quad\;\; |\, 0 \end{bmatrix} \\ \begin{bmatrix} [I - A_{11}(1)] \,|\, 0 \\ 0 \quad\;\; |\, 0 \end{bmatrix} B(0) \\ \begin{bmatrix} [I - A_{11}(k - 1)] \,|\, 0 \\ |\, 0 \end{bmatrix} \prod_t B(t) \end{bmatrix} \qquad t = 0, \ldots, k - 2 \qquad 4.11$$

This is of rank m at most, since the rank of the product matrix cannot exceed the rank of each factor matrix. The system is not, therefore, observable.

Similarly, let the control variables of the system be selected from the same vector of control outputs, but assume that the agents of the economy have the option of disposing of residuals as waste. In other words, let $j_i(t) \leq q_i(t) - q(t)a_i(t - 1)$ for all $q_i(t) - q(t)a_i(t - 1) > 0$, $i \in \{1, \ldots, m\}$. The $kn \times n$ controllability matrix, $J(k)$, is also of rank m at most:

$$J(k) = \begin{bmatrix} B(0) \begin{bmatrix} M(0)] \,|\, 0 \\ 0 \quad |\, 0 \end{bmatrix} \\ \begin{bmatrix} M(1)] \,|\, 0 \\ 0 \quad |\, 0 \end{bmatrix} \\ \cdots\cdots\cdots\cdots\cdots \\ \prod_t B(t) \begin{bmatrix} M(k - 1)] \,|\, 0 \\ 0 \quad\;\; |\, 0 \end{bmatrix} \end{bmatrix} \qquad t = 0, \ldots, k - 2 \qquad 4.12$$

The vector $j(0,k)J(k)$ is also positive in, at most, its first m components, implying that the last $n - m$ resources in the system are not touched directly by the controls.

The central point here is fairly obvious. If a subsystem within the general system has access to a limited set of observations on the state of the general system, and if it controls the output of only a limited set of resources, then it cannot determine the performance of the general system. The implications of this point are, perhaps, less obvious.

As we have already seen, the agents of a human economy comprising one of a number of mutually dependent subsystems may relieve the environmental constraints to the growth of that economy either by regulation of the level of capacity utilization, or by technological change. The first option should, by now, be well understood. It represents a type of control called by Kornai and Martos (1981) "control based on stock signals," and it is the most widespread and basic form of control. Control by stock signals is described as "vegetative control" which, they claim, has the following interesting properties: "it always takes place at the lowest level between producers and consumers, without intervention of higher administrative organizations. It is autonomous, i.e., not directly connected to any social process. . . . In control based on stock signals, the firm or household, only watch their own stock levels" (1981, pp. 60–61). Actually, as we will see later, social control by stock signals is not uncommon, but this is sufficient to demonstrate what is involved in this form of control.

The dominant feature is the adjustment of the level of activity of a process to satisfy or anticipate a constraint on the supply of one or more inputs to that process, or to meet excess demand for the outputs of that process. In both cases, the signal is the level of stocks in the controlled process. It is a form of control that is accordingly associated with technologically stationary processes, or at least with noninventive moments in the evolution of a technologically time-variant process. It is a response that seeks only to adapt to the limitations of the existing technology. Control by stock signals is also, in general, associated with non-expansionary systems. Where the stocks in question are interpreted as environmental resources, it can be read as a technique for adapting a process to the limits of the environment, rather than for bending the environment to fit the requirements of the process.

It is worth remarking that so long as the observations available are limited to the immediate performance of a subset of the processes undertaken in the human economy only, the general system will remain unobservable. If the system is unobservable, the application of residuals as control measures will have indeterminate effects beyond the controlled processes. That is, technological change informed by a system of signals based on the existence of residuals in the economy and limited to intervention within the economy cannot have determinate effects in the environment. Moreover, wherever the economy and the environment are mutually dependent, such technological change cannot have determinate effects even in respect to the economy. Unless the technology matrices decompose, there will be feedback effects caused by changes in the nature and level of waste disposal under the new technologies, and these will not be knowable in advance. It is, in fact, only if the economy and its environment are disjoint (a contradiction in terms) that technological change associated with the disposal of economic residuals will produce no unanticipated effects.

4.5   The paradox of growth

In contrast to the conservative approach implied by control by stock signals, the second option in the relief of the environmental constraints to growth, technological change, supposes an aggressive posture toward the environment. It implies not just change in the relative magnitudes of the input and output coefficients in a given process, but an extension of control over the resources of the environment. To see this, consider the processes of the economy described by the submatrices $\mathbf{A}_{11}(k)$, $\mathbf{A}_{12}(k)$, and $\mathbf{B}_{11}(k)$ in 4.1. For all these processes the conservation of mass implies, first, that $\underline{\mathbf{a}}_i(k)\mathbf{e} = \underline{\mathbf{b}}_i(k)\mathbf{e}$ for all $i \in \{1, \ldots, m\}$: the mass of inputs is exactly equal to the mass of outputs. What this means is that the mass of the jth resource produced in the ith process can exceed the mass of the jth resource used in the ith process only if the mass of some other resource is reduced. That is $b_{ij}(k) > a_{ij}(k)$ implies that $b_{ih}(k) < a_{ih}(k)$ for at least one $h \in \{1, \ldots, j - 1, j + 1, \ldots, n\}$. Notice, too, that the conservation of mass condition implies that if the output of any one process in the system is rising, then the output of some other process must be falling. That is, $\underline{\mathbf{b}}_i(k)\mathbf{e}/\underline{\mathbf{b}}_i(k - 1)\mathbf{e} > 1$, $i \in \{1, \ldots, n\}$, implies that $\underline{\mathbf{b}}_j(k)\mathbf{e}/\underline{\mathbf{b}}_j(k - 1)\mathbf{e} < 1$ for at least one $j \in \{1, \ldots, i - 1, i + 1, \ldots, n\}$.

Now output of the ith process may be said to be environmentally constrained – by shortage of the environmental resources required in production – wherever $q_h(k) < \mathbf{q}(k)\mathbf{a}_h(k - 1)$ for at least one $h \in \{m + 1, \ldots, n \mid a_{ih}(k) > 0\}$. That is, output in the ith process may be said to be environmentally constrained if, under the inherited technology, there is excess demand for at least one environmental resource used in the ith process. We are interested in the implications of possible adjustments to a binding environmental constraint.

If the agents controlling the ith process adjust by reducing the level of activity, output will fall. If they adjust the technology employed in the process so as to reduce the quantity required of the resource in excess demand by substituting some (observable) economic resource in excess supply, then output may be increased up to the point where all (observable) resources are fully utilized. That is, the elements $a_{ij}(k)$, $j = 1, \ldots, m$, may be increased to the point where $\mathbf{q}_1(k) = \mathbf{q}_1(k)\mathbf{A}_{11}(k)$. However, $\underline{\mathbf{b}}_j(k)\mathbf{e} > \underline{\mathbf{b}}_j(k - 1)\mathbf{e}$ only if $\mathbf{a}_i(k)\mathbf{e} > \mathbf{a}_i(k - 1)\mathbf{e}$. The potential rate of expansion in the physical output of the jth process will increase only if there is a net increase in the mass of resources advanced in the ith process. But note that the conservation of mass condition ensures that if the (full employment) rate of expansion in the physical output of any one process within the economy is increasing, while the quantity of environmental resources employed is contracting, then it will be at the expense of other processes in the economy. That is, if $\mathbf{b}_i(k)\mathbf{e} > \mathbf{b}_i(k - 1)\mathbf{e}$ while $\mathbf{a}_{ih}(k) < \mathbf{a}_{ih}(k - 1)$ for all $h \in \{m + 1, \ldots\ n\}$, then $\mathbf{a}_{ij}(k) > \mathbf{a}_{ij}(k - 1)$ and $\mathbf{b}_j(k)\mathbf{e} < \mathbf{b}_j(k - 1)\mathbf{e}$ for at least one $j \in \{1, \ldots, m\}$. Consequently, if the rate of expansion in physical output of all processes in the economy is to increase in the face of a binding environmental constraint, the quantity of substitute environmental resources advanced in those processes will have to be increased.

In terms of our description of technological change as a control process, if controlled technological change is to permit an increase in the growth of physical output in the economy, it must be possible to secure an increased flow of resources through the application of residuals. Since, as we have seen, the application of economic residuals to the economy is inconsistent with an increase in the rate of growth of the economy as a whole so long as the quantity of natural resources employed is declining, this implies that the range of control must be extended. In other words, if a binding environmental constraint is not to cause a slowdown in the physical rate of growth of the economy, more resources must be brought under economic control. In the language of control theory, more of the state variables will have to be made dependent on the control variables. The number of processes subject to the control of economic agents will have to be increased.

We are led, therefore, to a conclusion that is rather startling, at least on the surface. For technological change to offer relief to the environmental constraints to the physical growth of human economies, it is necessary to extend the range of human control – to bring new resources into the production of economic goods. The key to economic growth is the commercialization of new areas. But as the range of human control nears the limit, the conservation of mass condition imposes a more and more rigid constraint on the physical expansion of the economy. Hence, we have the paradox of growth: growth may continue providing that we learn how to control the resources of the globe, but if we learn how to control the resources of the globe, growth will no longer be possible.

This conclusion implies two things. First, the relief of the environmental constraints to growth is not simply a matter of throwing more resources at the problem. Second, it is meaningful to talk about the absolute scarcity of resources. There is some cause to doubt the notion that greater environmental control is a sufficient condition for the growth of human economies – at least for the 100 million years cited by Beckerman (1972, p. 338). There is some cause, too, to doubt the conviction of Brooks and Andrews (1974) that it is nonsensical to entertain the notion that we might actually run out of minerals. To understand why, however, we need to go beyond the simple logic of the model discussed in the last three chapters.

The supposition that environmental resources are physically non-scarce derives from the fact that the mass of the outputs of the economy is insignificant relative to the mass of the resources of the environment. It is argued that some resources may be more inaccessible than others, in which case they are relatively scarce. But in general there is enough of everything in store that we can continue to run stocks down for a good long time. Moreover, when we have finished off resources in situ, we can begin to recycle what has already been extracted. There is, however, a problem with this veiw, and it is one that has been argued with remarkable vigor and persistence by Georgescu-Roegen over a number of years (see, in particular, 1971, 1977, 1979).

Like energy, not all matter is available for exploitation, and like energy matter is continuously degrading from available to unavailable forms. In Georgescu-Roegen's own terms:

All over the material world there is rubbing by friction, cracking and splitting by changes in temperature or evaporation, there is clogging of pipes and membranes, there is metal fatigue and spontaneous combustion. Matter is thus continuously displaced, altered, and scattered to the four corners of the world. It thus becomes less and less available for our own purposes.

The energetic dogma claims that this dissipation can be completely reversed providing there is enough available energy. But the operation must necessarily involve some material instruments. Because there are no perdurable material structures these instruments will necessarily wear out. They will have to be produced by others produced by some other instruments, which will also wear out and will have to be replaced, and so on, in an unending regress. This regress is sufficient ground for denying the possibility of complete recycling, just as the same kind of regress is the reason often invoked in thermodynamics against the possibility of completely erasing the changes caused in the energy structure by natural process (1979; p. 1034).

Even if the outputs of the economy were not growing, it follows that it would be necessary to bite deeper and deeper into the resources of the environment. Moreover, the lower the durability of those resources, and the lower their entropy, the higher the rate of extraction required to maintain a given level of activity. The impossibility of recycling implies that the growth of output and the depletion of environmental resources in relatively fixed supply are synonymous.

For this very practical reason resource economists must entertain a theory of exhaustible resources, despite a conviction that the absolute scarcity of matter does not exist. It is by adding the assumption of perfect long-period substitutability that they can regard the exhaustion of any particular resource with equanimity. The permanent loss of a particular species or mineral is obviously of no account if there are other species or minerals with identical characteristics waiting in the wings. But as Georgescu-Roegen has reminded us, where energy and mass are homogeneous, matter is highly heterogeneous. "Every chemical element has at least one property that characterizes it completely and hence renders it indispensable for some technical recipes" (1979, p. 1035). Recalling that it was the complementarity of inputs that underpinned the results of the Doomsday Models, it is easy to see that this uniqueness of matter is extremely important. The exhaustion of any one resource impels a change both in the technology by which resources dependent on its use are produced and in the character of those resources. Substitution under the uniqueness of matter implies substitution of technologies. The disappearance of one of a number of complementary inputs automatically makes the other redundant.

PART II

The economic system

CHAPTER 5

The price system

5.1   Value in general

The physical system described in Part I includes a number of informationally distinct subsystems, with a subsystem said to be informationally distinct if it generates and responds to a set of signals different from the signals generated by all remaining subsystems. Although each informationally distinct subsystem may be technically dependent on all others, it operates on the basis of a separate set of signals. It has a separate identity. The human economies are among these informationally distinct subsystems.

As a first approximation, a human economy was defined in Section 1.2 to be a physical system of production organized according to a social set of signals. More particularly, it is a set of mutually dependent processes designed to satisfy an arbitrary range of human wants within the constraints of existing knowledge and resources, and organized according to a common set of signals. The basis of these signals is the value system, where the *value* of a resource is defined to be a corresponding transaction weight fixed by the conditions of production, distribution, and exchange. In classical terms, value is "value in exchange." We are not interested in the utility or use value of resources, although it is taken as axiomatic that resources will command a positive price only if they yield positive utility at the margin. Positive marginal utility is, however, necessary but not sufficient to ensure that a resource commands a positive price. The *value system* is defined to be the set of transaction weights governing the exchange of resources between the agents controlling the mutually dependent processes of a human economy. The value system is thus coextensive with the market.

Note that these definitions are very general. They say nothing either about the size and complexity of the economy or about the monetization of the system of signals. The mutual dependence of processes implies only that the gross input matrix describing the allocation of resources between processes is indecomposable. Each process is directly or indirectly a supplier of all other processes. The definition of the value system does not imply that the different processes should be at any particular distance from one another, nor does it prescribe the nature of the property rights in the system. There is nothing in the definition of the value system that necessarily sustains the distinction between "commodity economy," in which production is held to be for exchange, and "natural economy," in which production is held to be for use (cf. Lange, 1971). The extent of the division of labor is immaterial. All that is important is that enough of a division of labor exists to permit gains from the (interpersonal) trade of the services of resources subject to clear rights of property. Both an integrated commodity economy and the individual autonomous households of the natural economy will have their own value systems. The existence of common or communal property rights is quite compatible with a well-defined value system so long as the usufructuary rights of those with access to the common or communal property are reasonably well defined.

Similarly, the definition of value implies only the existence of some basis for the weights commanded by resources in exchange. It has nothing to say about the Aristotelian distinction between economies dominated by monetary calculation and those in which calculation is argued to be nonmonetary. The existence of a unit of account is irrelevant to the valorization of resources. The value system is any system of weights establishing the ratio in which resources, defined in terms of property rights, are exchanged one for another. It does not matter whether an exchange is based on gift and ceremony, barter, money barter, or money, so long as the parties to the transaction are mutually dependent.

5.2   Elements of the price system

The analysis of this and subsequent chapters is conducted at a somewhat lower level of abstraction than is implied by this very general description of the value. More particularly, the referent system is taken to be a market economy in which agents have individual or joint property in the resources employed in the system, and in which the value of a resource is given by its relative price. Resource prices are determined in a competitive process that respects the law of supply and demand, but that also reflects a contest over the distribution of income. The key elements in the determination of prices are thus: (1) the relative scarcity of resources in terms of the technology applying to both their production and use, and (2) a contest between the owners of complementary factors of production over the distribution of income. To the five core assumptions about the nature of the physical system described in Section 2.1 we may thus add the following two core assumptions about the nature of the price system.

Assumption 6: The exchange values or prices of economic resources are determined by the conditions of both production and distribution. The conditions of production, it should be recalled, are given by the technology of the system, where technology is defined as the pool of knowledge that bounds all the material transformations of the global system. Technology therefore includes both the preference sets of the agents of the system and the set of available techniques of production in economic activities: the activities of households are described in the rows of the technology matrices in the same way as the activities of firms are. The conditions of production describe both the supply and demand potentials of the system. The conditions of distribution refer to the extra-economic – cultural, legal, ideological, and political – conditions affecting the distribution of income between the proprietors of distinct factors of production. This assumption gives formal recognition to the fact that there is a noneconomic component in the (functional) distribution of income, and that this is reflected in relative prices.

Assumption 7: In any given interval in the history of an economy there exists a high degree of complementarity between various well-defined groups of resources. These resources constitute the factors of production. Economic production is held to be cooperative, in the sense that it involves the proprietors of two or more complementary factors. This complementarity of factors of production underpins the distributional contest. If all factors of production were perfectly substitutable, returns to each would be driven to equality. It is only because factors are not perfectly substitutable that the distributional contest is of interest.

The classical arbitrage condition is that all property advanced by capitalists, that is, all capital, should attract the same return. This reflects the driving force of competition in the capitalist economy in the face of fluctuations in market prices: Ricardo's "restless desire on the part of all employers of stock to quit a less profitable for a more advantageous business, [which] has a strong tendency to equalize the rate of profits for all" (1951, p. 88). The same competitive process applies to the proprietors of other factors of production and will be sufficient to ensure the equalization of rates of return to those factors of production, but notice that it is not assumed that the return on factors of production other than capital should yield the same return as that on capital.

It is worth noting, in parentheses, that a conflict over the returns to property between the proprietors of distinct classes of inputs implies collusion between the members of each class of proprietor. It implies class action. This is strikingly similar to what might be called the fundamental proposition of Marxian distribution theory, which is that conflict over the distribution of the product in societies resting on the separation of property in the means of production takes the form of class conflict. Since the suppliers of a particular class of commodities will be indifferent between processes using their commodities only if the return is the same for all processes, no one proprietor can secure a higher return than any other. Any action that changes the rate of return on a particular commodity must involve all the proprietors of that commodity. In other words, it will be a class action. Accordingly, the economic actors of interest are not individuals per se, but the group of proprietors of each set of perfectly substitutable resources advanced in production. If a perfectly substitutable set of resources is owned by a number of agents, it is the behavior of the group and not of the individuals within the group that is of interest. If each of the resources in an n-dimensional system is owned by more than one agent, we will be concerned with, at most, n distributive variables.

In order to explore the implications of these core assumptions, this chapter abstracts from the problem of the joint determination of the economic and environmental systems by making the same very powerful environmental assumptions that underpin modern classical general equilibrium theory. Although the main concern of this book is the importance of the price system in the relation between the economy and its environment, it is assumed, for the moment, that all resources produced in the system are valorized. This supposes that all processes in the system are in the control of human agents responding to the same set of signals, and are subject to well-defined property rights. In addition, it is assumed that the economy is capable of physical expansion or contraction under the protection of both the free gifts and the free disposal assumptions. The economy enjoys unlimited supplies of environmental resources, and can freely dispose of any wastes.

The justification for making these environmental assumptions is that they enable us to abstract from the all-important effects of evolutionary change. In the real world, commodity prices are carriers of information on the state of the system at any given moment in time. The information they contain is of an essentially transient nature. As

Shackle has reminded us, "There is no constant, permeable, isolable thing called 'value,' there are only the ratios in which goods exchange in the circumstances of the particular day and hour on the market. Market values are the solutions of the practical task of pre-reconciliation of actions. They are signals and expressions of a situation in which tastes or needs, endowments, expectations are the real elements, elements which are some of them ephemeral" (1972, p. 112). The purpose of this chapter is to explore the properties of the price system as an information system independently of any fluctuations in these "real elements" of the system. By abstracting from the evolutionary, ever-changing nature of the physical system we can disentangle the technological, political, and economic effects on the price signals of a given system. But it should not be thought that these assumptions are offered as approximations – first or otherwise – of economic systems existing in historical time. Actual economies cannot rely on the free gifts of nature or the free disposal of wastes, and cannot avoid fluctuations in the real elements of the system. The existence of excess demand will call for adjustments in both the price and quantity systems. To bring out the properties of the former, however, this chapter ignores the latter.

To begin let us define two vectors: $\mathbf{p}(k)$ is a time indexed n-dimensional column vector of prices. Since all resources are assumed to be positively valued it is strictly positive. $p_i(k)$ is the price of the ith resource in the kth period. $\mathbf{r}(k)$ is a strictly positive time indexed n-dimensional column vector of process revenues. $r_i(k)$ indicates the value of output of the ith process in the kth period. These two vectors are related by the equation

$$
\begin{bmatrix} r_1 \\ \vdots \\ r_n \end{bmatrix} (k)
$$

$$
= \begin{bmatrix} q_1 & & 0 \\ & \ddots & \\ 0 & & q_n \end{bmatrix} (k-1) \begin{bmatrix} b_{11} & \cdots & b_{1n} \\ \vdots & & \vdots \\ b_{1n} & \cdots & b_{nn} \end{bmatrix} (k-1) \begin{bmatrix} p_1 \\ \vdots \\ p_n \end{bmatrix} (k)
$$

$$5.1$$

or, compactly,

$$
\mathbf{r}(k) = D\mathbf{q}(k-1)\mathbf{B}(k-1)\mathbf{p}(k) \qquad 5.2
$$

Equations 5.1 and 5.2 simply say that $r_i(k)$ is equal to the sum of the value of all outputs produced by the ith process in the $k-1$th period.

$r_i(k)$ thus indicates the revenue available to the proprietor(s) of the ith process at the commencement of the kth period.

The essential feature of models built on the assumption of the complementarity of the main factors of production is that there is no mechanism to ensure the equalization of returns to all factors. Consequently, if we admit that there are institutionally distinct classes of proprietor advancing inputs to a system resting on private property in the means of production, and if we assume that there is strictly limited substitutability between the inputs advanced by each class of proprietor, then there will be as many distributive variables as there are classes. In the extreme case, there will be n distributive variables describing the institutionally and market determined returns to the n proprietors or classes of proprietor in the system. These distributive variables comprise the diagonal elements of the time-indexed matrix of "rents":

$$\mathbf{Dw}(k) = \begin{bmatrix} w_1 & 0 & \cdots & 0 \\ 0 & w_2 & \cdots & 0 \\ \vdots & \vdots & & \vdots \\ 0 & 0 & \cdots & w_n \end{bmatrix} (k) \qquad 5.3$$

in which $w_i(k)$ is greater than, less than, or equal to zero as the proprietor of the ith resource earns, respectively, a positive, zero, or negative rate of return in the kth period. By *assumption 7* $w_i(k) \neq w_j(k)$ for at least one $i \neq j \in \{1, \ldots, n\}$, and for all $k \geq 0$. $\mathbf{Dw}(k)$ is located on the right of the gross input matrix. Hence $w_i(k)$ scales the ith column of $A(k)$. $\mathbf{Dw}(k)$ thus reflects the condition for the proprietor(s) of a particular input (class of inputs) to be indifferent between processes; namely, that the return should be the same in all processes.

By *assumption 6* the value of the outputs of all processes is held to be equal to the value of the inputs to those processes, with each input marked up by the rate of return on the class of inputs to which it belongs. That is,

$$\begin{bmatrix} r_1 \\ \vdots \\ r_n \end{bmatrix} (k) = \begin{bmatrix} q_1 & & 0 \\ & \ddots & \\ 0 & & q_n \end{bmatrix} (k-1) \begin{bmatrix} a_{11} & \cdots & a_{1n} \\ \vdots & & \vdots \\ a_{1n} & \cdots & a_{nn} \end{bmatrix} (k-1)$$

$$\begin{bmatrix} 1+w_1 & & 0 \\ & \ddots & \\ 0 & & 1+w_n \end{bmatrix} (k-1) \begin{bmatrix} p_1 \\ \vdots \\ p_n \end{bmatrix} (k-1) \qquad 5.4$$

or, compactly,

$$\mathbf{r}(k) = \mathbf{Dq}(k - 1)\mathbf{A}(k - 1)[\mathbf{I} + \mathbf{Dw}(k - 1)]\mathbf{p}(k - 1) \qquad 5.5$$

Substituting 5.2 into 5.5 and premultiplying each by the inverse of $\mathbf{Dq}(k - 1)$ reduces this to

$$\mathbf{B}(k - 1)\mathbf{p}(k) = \mathbf{A}(k - 1)[\mathbf{I} + \mathbf{Dw}(k - 1)]\mathbf{p}(k - 1) \qquad 5.6$$

These are the fundamental price equations of the system.

5.3   Prices of production

We may now consider the dynamic properties of such a system in terms of the particular assumptions of this chapter, taking separately the influence of technical conditions and the market. To describe the influence of the technical conditions of production on the price system, we may make the additional interim assumption that the distributive variables are fixed exogenously at a common rate, and that the system is technologically stationary. This combination of assumptions enables us to home in on the relation between relative prices and a given technique of production. The resulting set of prices are those referred to by the classical political economists as *prices of production:* "the prices which obtain as the average of the various rates of profit in the different spheres of production added to the cost-prices of the different spheres of production" (Marx, 1974, p. 157). In other words they are the prices struck once a uniform rate of profit exists and the market has cleared; what Marx described as "the centres around which the daily market prices fluctuate and tend to equalize one another within definite periods" (1974, p. 179).

To begin, let us go over some old ground – the necessary and sufficient conditions for the stability of the price set associated with any given technology. The vector of prices, $\mathbf{p}(k)$, may be said to be stable if, for any initial values for $p_i(0)$, $i \in \{1, \dots, n\}$, $\lim_{k\to\infty} p_i(k) = p_i^*$ (a constant) for all i. It may be said to be relatively stable if $\lim_{k\to\infty} p_i(k)/p_i(k - 1) = \sigma$ for all i, where σ is a positive scalar. That is, the vector of prices may be said to be stable if, as k tends to infinity, each of the components of $\mathbf{p}(k)$ converges to a constant value; and relatively stable if, as k tends to infinity, each component of $\mathbf{p}(k)$ increases or decreases at the same rate.

By the assumption of this section the rate of return on all inputs is equal. That is, $w_i(k) = w_j(k)$ for all $i,j \in \{1, \dots, n\}$ and for all $k \geq 0$. We can readily see that in a closed, input indecomposable, technologically stationary system described by the n-square pair $\mathbf{A,B}$, if $\mathbf{B}^{-1}\mathbf{A}$ is nonnegative, the price vector will converge to a stable positive vector if and only if the uniform rate of return is less than or equal to the Sraffa-Neumann equilibrium rate of profit.

The Sraffa-Neumann rate of profit in a price system of the form in 5.6 is obtained from the inverse of the dominant eigenvalue of the matrix $\mathbf{B}^{-1}\mathbf{A}$ (Abraham-Frois and Berrebi, 1979). If we define $\mathbf{B}^{-1}\mathbf{A} = \mathbf{C}$, and if we denote the Sraffa-Neumann equilibrium rate of profit by w^*, then if $w_i(k) = w^*$ for all $i \in \{1, \ldots, n\}$ and for all $k \geq 0$, $\lim_{k \to \infty} \mathbf{p}(k) = \mathbf{p}^* > 0$ if $(1 + w^*) = 1/\lambda_{max}(\mathbf{C})$, where $\lambda_{max}(\mathbf{C})$ is the dominant eigenvalue of $\mathbf{C}$.

It is worth noting two things about the assumptions being made here. First, the assumption that $\mathbf{B}^{-1}\mathbf{A}$ is nonnegative is very strong if there is joint production or fixed capital. Second, the assumption that $\mathbf{B}$ is nonsingular implies that every process produces a distinct set of outputs: that is, it is not possible to generate the outputs of any one process by scaling or combining the outputs of other processes. The nonsingularity of $\mathbf{B}$ implies that it is of full rank (its rows and columns are linearly independent).

The proof is straightforward and, by now, familiar. Since the system is time invariant, since $\mathbf{B}$ is nonsingular, and since $w_i(k) = w^*$ for all $i \in \{1, \ldots, n\}$ and for all $k \geq 0$, we may write 5.6 in the form

$$\mathbf{p}(k) = \mathbf{C}(1 + w^*)\mathbf{p}(k - 1) \qquad 5.7$$

$\mathbf{C}$ is indecomposable and nonnegative by assumption. There accordingly exists a nonsingular matrix $\mathbf{S}$, and so a matrix $\mathbf{T} = \mathbf{S}^{-1}$, such that

$$\mathbf{C} = \mathbf{S}\mathbf{D}\lambda\mathbf{T} \qquad 5.8$$

in which $\mathbf{D}\lambda = $ diagonal $\{\lambda_1, \ldots, \lambda_n\}$ is the set of eigenvalues of $\mathbf{C}$, ordered such that $\lambda_1 = \lambda_{max}(\mathbf{C})$. The rows and columns of $\mathbf{T}$ and $\mathbf{S}$ are the eigenvectors of $\mathbf{C}$. More particularly, the first row of $\mathbf{T}$, $\underline{t}_1$ and the first column of $\mathbf{S}$, $\mathbf{s}_1$ are, respectively, the left and right eigenvectors of $\mathbf{C}$ corresponding to $\lambda_{max}(\mathbf{C})$. By the Perron-Frobenius theorem each is strictly positive.

The general solution of 5.7 is

$$\mathbf{p}(k) = [\mathbf{C}(1 + w^*)]^k \mathbf{p}(0) \qquad 5.9$$

which, from 5.8 we may write, in the limit, as

$$\lim_{k \to \infty} \mathbf{p}(k) = \mathbf{S}\mathbf{D}[\lambda(1 + w^*)]^k \mathbf{T}\mathbf{p}(0) \qquad 5.10$$

This is symmetrical to 2.9. Sufficiency follows directly. If $(1 + w^*) = 1/\lambda_{max}(\mathbf{C})$, then, from the ordering of $\mathbf{D}\lambda$, we have in the limit $\lim_{k \to \infty} \mathbf{D}\lambda(1 + w^*)^k = \mathbf{D}[1, 0, \ldots, 0]$.

Hence, 5.10 can be written in the form

$$\lim_{k\to\infty}\mathbf{p}(k) = \mathbf{SD}[1,0,\ldots,0]\mathbf{Tp}(0) \qquad 5.11$$

Recall that $\mathbf{s}_1$ is a positive right eigenvector of $\mathbf{C}$ corresponding to $\lambda_{max}(\mathbf{C})$, and is therefore defined up to a scalar multiple. Since $\mathbf{D}[1,0,\ldots,0]\mathbf{Tp}(0)$ is a column vector the first component of which is positive and all other components are zero, $\mathbf{p}(k)$ converges in the limit to a positive right eigenvector of $\mathbf{C}$ of constant absolute value.

To see necessity let $(1 + w^*) \neq 1/\lambda_{max}(\mathbf{C})$. If $1/\lambda_i(\mathbf{C}) > (1 + w^*) > 1/\lambda_{max}(\mathbf{C})$, $i \in \{2,\ldots,n\}$, then $\lim_{k\to\infty}\mathbf{D}\lambda(1 + w^*)^k = \mathbf{D}[\infty,0,\ldots,0]$ which is undefined. If $1/\lambda_i(\mathbf{C}) < (1 + w^*) > 1/\lambda_{max}(\mathbf{C})$, $i \in \{2,\ldots,n\}$, then $\lim_{k\to\infty}\mathbf{D}\lambda(1 + w^*)^k = \mathbf{D}[0,0,\ldots,0]$. Hence $\lim_{k\to\infty}\mathbf{p}(k)$ is not stable for any $(1 + w^*) \neq 1/\lambda_{max}(\mathbf{C})$.

Notice, though, that it is possible to show that that prices will be relatively stable even if they are explosively inflating or deflating. That is, all prices will be rising or falling at the same rate. From 5.10 the ratio $p_i(k)/p_i(k-1)$ is in the limit

$$\lim_{k\to\infty}\frac{p_i(k)}{p_i(k-1)} \qquad 5.12$$
$$= \frac{[\lambda_1(1 + w^*)]^k\mathbf{SD}\{[\lambda_1(1 + w^*)]^{-1}\lambda(1 + w^*)\}^k\mathbf{Tp}(0)\mathbf{e}_i}{[\lambda_1(1 + w^*)]^{k-1}\mathbf{SD}\{[\lambda_1(1 + w^*)]^{-1}\lambda(1 + w^*)\}^{k-1}\mathbf{Tp}(0)\mathbf{e}_i}$$

for all $i \in \{1,\ldots,n\}$, where $\mathbf{e}_i$ is the ith unit vector. Since both $\mathbf{D}\{[\lambda_1(1 + w^*)]^{-1}\lambda(1 + w^*)\}^k$ and $\mathbf{D}\{[\lambda_1(1 + w^*)]^{-1}\lambda(1 + w^*)\}^{k-1}$ converge to $\mathbf{D}[1,0,\ldots,0]$ as k tends to infinity, we have

$$\lim_{k\to\infty}p_i(k)/p_i(k-1) = \lambda_1(1 + w^*) \qquad 5.13$$

for all $i \in \{1,\ldots,n\}$.

The stability of prices of production under the assumptions of this section depend on the magnitude of the uniform rate of return. In the case where the uniform rate of return is equal to the Sraffa-Neumann equilibrium rate of profit, absolute prices – the price level – will be stable. In all other cases, prices will be relatively stable, with the price structure determined by the technical conditions of production alone. Providing that the particular arbitrage conditions assumed here have been satisfied, the spectral properties of the technology matrices determine relative prices at equilibrium. Notice, though, that this result is highly sensitive to the arbitrage conditions assumed. Once we relax the assumption that returns to all inputs are equalized, the influence of the technical conditions of production on relative prices is reduced.

5.4   The price level under multiple rates of return

To approach the analysis of the general price system in a multifactor, multiclass disequilibrium system, consider the determinants of both relative prices and the price level where there are multiple rates of return. We have seen that relative prices (of production) may be stable for a range of uniform rates of return under the classical arbitrage condition, but that the price level is stable only if the uniform rate of return is equal to the Sraffa-Neumann equilibrium rate of profit. It can now be shown that the convergence of the price level under a given technology is quite consistent with multiple rates of return. However, where multiple rates of return exist, the role of technology in determining relative prices turns out to be substantially weakened.

To see this let us persist with the assumption, for the moment, that the returns on all inputs are time-invariant. Hence, $\mathbf{w}(k) = \mathbf{w}$ for all $k \geq 0$. Recall that the upper and lower bounds for the dominant eigenvalue of an indecomposable nonnegative matrix are given by the maximum and minimum column sums of the matrix (Gantmacher, 1959, p. 76). Hence, the upper and lower bounds for the dominant eigenvalue of $\mathbf{C}$ are its maximum and minimum column sums. These may be defined as $\mathbf{ec}_{max}$ and $\mathbf{ec}_{min}$, where $\mathbf{e}$, as before, is a unit (summing) vector. Now if absolute prices are convergent, then in the limit

$$\lim_{k \to \infty} \mathbf{p}(k) = \mathbf{C}[\mathbf{I} + \mathbf{Dw}]\mathbf{p}(k-1) = \mathbf{p}^* \qquad 5.14$$

An invariant $\mathbf{p}^*$ implies that the dominant eigenvalue of the matrix $\mathbf{C}[\mathbf{I} + \mathbf{Dw}]$ in 5.13 has an absolute value of unity. Since a sufficient condition for this is to be true is that $\mathbf{ec}_i = 1$ for all $i \in \{1, \ldots, n\}$, wherever $\mathbf{ec}_{max} \neq \mathbf{ec}_{min}$, there exists a vector $\mathbf{w}^* = [w_1^*, \ldots, w_n^*]$, with $w_i^* \neq w_j^*$ for at least one $i,j \in \{1, \ldots, n\}$, such that $\mathbf{ec}_i w_i^* = 1$. w_i^* will be positive for all i only if $\mathbf{ec}_{max} < 1$; that is, there will be a positive return on all classes of input only if all columns of $\mathbf{C}$ sum to less than unity. The implications of this for the price level and for relative prices are immediate.

The first thing to note is that the properties of the sociotechnological matrix, $\mathbf{F} = \mathbf{B}^{-1}\mathbf{A}[\mathbf{I} + \mathbf{Dw}]$, and not the technological matrix, $\mathbf{C} = \mathbf{B}^{-1}\mathbf{A}$, are important in determining the price level. Since $\mathbf{p}(k) = \lambda_{max}(\mathbf{F})\mathbf{p}(k-1)$ as k tends to infinity, if the dominant eigenvalue of $\mathbf{F}$ is greater than unity, the time path of prices will be explosively inflating in the limit; if it is less than unity, prices will be collapsing. In other words, if claims to the net product exceed the technologically determined capacity of the system to produce a surplus, then the price level will be rising. If claims fall short of the capacity of the system to deliver, then prices will be falling. $\lambda_{max}(\mathbf{F})$ thus defines what may be called the coefficient of the inflationary potential of a given technology and a given distribution of income.

In respect to the set of relative prices, what is important is that for k very large the price vector will come very close to an eigenvector of $\mathbf{F}$, implying that it is the spectral properties of the sociotechnological matrix that determine the relative prices of inputs, and not the properties of the technology matrix alone. Without the equalization of rates of return the price system is a product of both the technical and political conditions of the system. It is determined by the political economy of the system.

5.5   Market prices

We may now relax the assumption that the structure of the distribution vector, $\mathbf{w}(k)$, is constant for all $k \geq 0$. Consistent with *assumption 7*, rates of return on inputs will be allowed to vary with the level of excess demand for those inputs. Since quantity adjustments are precluded by assumption we will be considering only price responses. If we assume – with Ricardo and Marx – that the returns accruing to the seller of a commodity in a particular period are a function of the level of excess demand for the commodity in that period, then so long as the level of excess demand for all resources is not constant in all periods, the sociotechnological matrix $\mathbf{F}(k)$ will be time varying, even though in the absence of quantity adjustments the technology matrices $\mathbf{A}(k),\mathbf{B}(k)$ will be constant for all $k \geq 0$.

The excess demand for all commodities in the kth period in a technologically time-invariant system is described by the n-dimensional row vector $\mathbf{q}_E(k)$:

$$\mathbf{q}_E(k) = \mathbf{q}(k)[\mathbf{A} - \mathbf{I}] \qquad\qquad 5.15$$

from which it is clear that $\mathbf{q}(k) \neq \mathbf{q}(k + 1)$ implies that $\mathbf{q}_E(k) \neq \mathbf{q}_E(k + 1)$. Excess demand for the ith commodity in the kth period $q_{Ei}(k) = \mathbf{q}(k)\mathbf{a}_i - q_i(k)$ is greater than, equal to, or less than zero as the full capacity demand for the ith commodity is greater than, equal to, or less than the quantity available to the system at the period's commencement.

The dependence of the distributive variables on the level of excess demand implies a function of the general form

$$w_i(k) = f(q_{Ei}(k)),\ f' > 0 \qquad i = 1, \ldots, n \qquad\qquad 5.16$$

The classical link between fluctuations in the level of excess demand and the return on the ith commodity implies that the first derivatives of the function are positive. An increase (decrease) in the level of excess demand for the ith commodity is associated with an increase (decrease) in the return to the proprietors of that commodity. Moreover, because there is a direct relation between prices and the distributive variables $[\partial p_j(k + 1)/\partial w_i(k) > 0$ for all $i \in \{1, \ldots, n\}$ from 5.6], an increase in the excess demand for the ith commodity which increases the returns to the sellers of that commodity will necessarily raise the output prices of all processes employing the ith commodity.

From 5.14 it is immediate that the stability of a time-varying distribution vector is a necessary (though not a sufficient) condition for a technologically time-invariant system to have a zero inflationary potential. That is, $\lim_{k \to \infty} \mathbf{p}(k)\lambda_{\max}(\mathbf{F}) = \mathbf{C}[\mathbf{I} + \mathbf{D}\mathbf{w}(k)]\mathbf{p}(k) = \mathbf{p}^*$ only if $\lim_{k \to \infty} \mathbf{w}(k) = \mathbf{w}^*$, where $\mathbf{w}^*$ denotes any constant distribution vector satisfying this equation. If we consider the effects of excess demand on the distributive variables, then it is similarly immediate from 5.15 and 5.16 that a technologically time-invariant system will have a zero inflationary potential only if

$$\lim_{k \to \infty} w_i(k) = [\mathbf{q}(k)\mathbf{a}_i/q_i(k)]w_i^* = w_i^* \qquad 5.17$$

for all $i \in \{1, \ldots, n\}$. In other words, a necessary condition for the price stability of a technologically time-invariant system is that $w_i(k)$ converges to a full employment rate of return for all i. Under the special assumptions of this chapter the distribution vector may be convergent only if the vector of excess demands converges to zero; that is, only if, in the limit, all markets clear. A necessary condition for the physical system to satisfy 5.17 is, therefore, that $\lim_{k \to \infty} q_i(k) = \mathbf{q}(k)\mathbf{a}_i$ for all i. If $\mathbf{q}(k)$ is invariant under the transformation $\mathbf{q}(k)\mathbf{A}$ for any k, it is a left eigenvector of $\mathbf{A}$ corresponding to an eigenvalue of modulus one. Hence a necessary condition for the convergence of the vector of excess demands to zero is that the quantity vector converge to a left eigenvector of $\mathbf{A}$ corresponding to an eigenvalue equal to unity.

To summarize, the time path of the general price system in a technologically time-invariant economy has the form

$$\mathbf{B}\mathbf{p}(k + 1) = \mathbf{A}[\mathbf{I} + \mathbf{f}(\mathbf{q}_E(k))]\mathbf{p}(k) \qquad 5.18$$

the necessary conditions for the convergence of which are given by the pair of equations:

$$\lim_{k \to \infty} \mathbf{q}(k) = \mathbf{q}(k)[\mathbf{A} - \mathbf{I}] = 0 \qquad 5.19$$
$$\lim_{k \to \infty} \mathbf{C}[\mathbf{I} + \mathbf{D}\mathbf{w}(k)]\mathbf{p}(k) = \mathbf{F}(k)\mathbf{p}(k) = \mathbf{p}^*$$

5.19 implies that the system is both technologically capable of attaining a full employment (market-clearing) position, and that there exists an adjustment process by which the distributive variables respond to negative feedbacks from fluctuations in excess demands and the price level.

5.6   The range of price information

The real significance of *assumptions 6* and *7* is that the price signals carry information over and above the relative scarcity of resources. In the time-invariant systems discussed in this chapter there certainly exists a time path of prices generating increasingly precise information on the relative scarcity of resources resulting from the relative productivity of the processes yielding those resources. But the existence of multiple rates of return, "explained" by limited substitution possibilities under the technology of the system, implies that the relative magnitudes of the components of the price vector also carry information on the relative distributional claims of distinct classes of agent. Moreover, the price level signals the sustainability of aggregate claims to the net product, this being recorded in the coefficient of inflationary potential, the dominant eigenvalue of the sociotechnological matrix **F**.

The price system offers both economic and noneconomic information on the system. The distinction, cited earlier in this chapter, between commodity and natural economy, can now be seen as a distinction between value systems in which only the relative importance of economic and noneconomic factors is different. The price system in commodity economies reflects noneconomic distributional considerations just as the transaction weights in natural economies reflect the relative scarcity of resources. The price system in any political economy may be coextensive with the market, but it reflects much more than the simple operation of the law of supply and demand. Nor have we yet taken account of the existence of a physical environment to the physical processes of the economy. So long as our analysis is protected by the assumption of free gifts and free disposals – the assumptions of this chapter – the fact that the economy is embedded in a wider environment implies nothing of significance for the price system. Once we relax these assumptions, however, everything changes. Without free gifts and free disposals we cannot sustain our interim assumption of a technologically stationary economy. Using the price system as a guide, the agents of the economy not only can but must change the combination of resources employed in production, through innovation or invention. But then the process of price convergence under each new

technique of production will convey a sequence of sometimes contra-
dictory signals (since the convergence of each price will by no means
be monotonic) that may stimulate further inventions and further innovations. More important, without free gifts and disposals the physical
processes of the economy can no longer be regarded as isolated from
those of their environment, implying that change due to the time
behavior of the price signals will be associated with unsignalled or only
partially signalled change in the nature of economy-environment interactions. The forward or future information conveyed by the price system will be increasingly subject to uncertainty due to unnoticed environmental effects.

The question of future prices in an evolutionary system will be discussed later. In the meantime, as we edge closer to a description of the
market solution, it is worth recording that just as prices signal more
than the scarcity of resources in the economies of the real world, so the
scarcity of resources is signalled by more than prices. The concept of
human action does not, after all, imply any particular signals or any
particular form of calculation (which may happen to satisfy current
prejudices about what is or what is not economically rational). As von
Mises has argued, human action implies only a faithful response to
what are taken to be the signals of the system. It does not imply that
those signals are, in any objective way, right. "A peasant eager to get a
rich crop may," he points out, "choose various methods. He may perform some magical rites, he may embark upon a pilgrimage, he may
offer a candle to the image of his patron saint, or he may employ more
or better fertilizer. But whatever he does, it is always action, i.e., the
employment of means for the attainment of ends ... the concept of
action does not imply that the action is guided by a correct theory and
a technology promising of success and that it attains the end aimed at.
It only implies that the performer of the action believes that the means
applied will produce the desired effect" (1949, p. 37). In an uncertain
world, the cast of bones, aerial portents, and future market prices are
all members of the same genus, and may all be consulted by those anx-
ious to justify their guesses as to the future effects of current actions.

CHAPTER 6

Prices, property, and the environment

6.1   Property, possession, and control

The value system in any economy defines the weights in exchange of a given set of proprietary resources (assets) or, more properly, of the services deriving from those resources. The value system thus supposes a corresponding set of property rights. Once we come to look at the role of prices in an economy-environment system, we need to add that the set of property rights is characterized by a clear distinction between recognized (positively valued) and unrecognized (zero valued) rights. If a resource used in a human economy is zero valued, then it is exacted and is not subject to recognized property rights. If the same resource is positively valued, then it is transacted and subject to recognized property rights. So the distinction, for example, between slaves and free persons in human societies is that the former are not recognized as having rights of property over their various capacities, while the latter are. The labor of the slave is exacted; the labor of the free person is transacted.

The distinction between zero and positively valued resources rests first and foremost on a technical consideration. From equation 5.6 it follows that zero-valued resources are defined by the fact that they directly require no positively valued resource for their production. In other words, up to the point at which the exaction of a zero-valued resource occurs its production is directly independent of all positively valued resources. In contrast to this, positively valued resources are defined by the fact that they do directly require other positively valued resources for their production. This does not mean that the production of zero-valued resources is entirely unaffected by the activities yielding positively valued resources, since it leaves open the possibility of indirect effects through, for example, pollution. But as the fundamental price equations show, the price or unit value of any resource is a function of the price of the direct inputs in the process(es) producing that resource.

This provides an alternative perspective on the conventional distinction between economically nonscarce (zero-valued) and economically scarce (positively valued) resources. Resources are only economically nonscarce if they may be obtained without surrendering a positively valued resource in the process. Hence, resources that are susceptible to exaction are nonscarce. Conversely, resources are economically scarce when their utilization in the processes of a human economy implies the commitment of positively valued resources to secure their possession.

The term *possession* has a very precise meaning here. The commitment of positively valued resources to the exaction of environmental resources implies that the latter are possessed and so endowed with value. Possession, in this sense, is both a necessary and sufficient condition for an environmental resource to be positively valued. Proprietary rights in a process are, by contrast, necessary but not sufficient to ensure that the outputs of that process are positively valued. In general, however, the possession of a resource, and so its valorization, need not be exclusive. Possession of a resource by one agent, and so the valorization of that resource in terms of the price system that informs the behavior of that agent, does not imply that the same resource may not be possessed by other agents operating on the basis of a different set of signals. The possession of a resource implies that it is incorporated in a particular property and, hence, value system. Accordingly, the allocation of that resource depends on the signals of the value system informing its possessor. But if the same resource is possessed by agents operating on the basis of a different set of signals, the actual deployment of the resource depends on both sets of signals.

In terms of a given value system, however, property in a resource (or category of resources) gives the proprietor (or class of proprietors) the right to exclude others from that resource. Indeed, the most fundamental principle of private property in economic theory is the principle of exclusion. For possession to be generally exclusive, therefore, the value system in terms of which each resource is possessed has to be unique. This implies that all agents in the general physical system behave in accordance with a common set of signals. If it is not true that all agents dependent on a given set of resources respond to the same set of signals, then multiple possession of resources will exist. The allocation of resources will depend on two or more different sets of signals.

Historically, a multiplicity of value systems have existed. Where these value systems have overlapped, multiple possession of resources has occurred. What is important about the existence of multiple systems of signals, from the point of view of this essay, is that they indicate the limits of control in the relation between an economy and its environment. Although this problem received comparatively little attention until the second half of this century, at least insofar as it concerns the controllability of the natural environment, it has long been a concern of those exploring the problem of control in economy-human environment interactions. The relation between feudal landowner and tenant is a case in point. In his treatment of the genesis of capitalist ground rent Marx, for an early example, was at pains to point out that the serf in feudal agricultural systems was "in possession of his own means of production" and conducted "his agricultural activity and the rural home industries connected with it independently." In consequence, he argued, "the surplus labour for the nominal owner of the land can only be extorted from them by *other than economic pressure*" (1974, pp. 790–91; italics added). Slave, corvee, or tribute-based systems are similarly founded on a political relation of domination and subordination, rather than the mutual self-interest of agents meeting in the marketplace.

More recently, the frequent observation in the development literature that "development" has historically been inhibited by the persistence of archaic or traditional behavior among "backward" peoples reflects the same phenomenon. An often repeated assertion of the 1950s and 1960s was that a precondition for development was a revolution in the way in which people responded to economic signals. Leibenstein, for example, argued that: "it is necessary to create an outlook in which success is gauged by market performance and in which rational, rather than conventional or traditional considerations are the determinants of action" (1957, p. 110. Cf. also Rostow, 1960). Acceptance of the signals of the capitalist world market was equated with "rationality in cognition" (Kindleberger, 1965, p. 21). Absolute rationality and responsiveness to a particular, historically specific set of signals were confounded. In this, as Godelier (1972) points out, these authors were merely making the virtually universal assumption of the "rationality" of the modern capitalist system and of the "irrationality" of all noncapitalist systems. But the problem was not the ideological or psychological "backwardness" of peoples still responsive to signals other than market prices; instead, it was the uncontrollability of the human environment of the colonial economy by means other than force majeure.

The point is quite simply that if the generation and appropriation of surplus take place within a single market, it implies that resources will be allocated through a system of transactions between mutually dependent processes. If this does not take place within a single market, then it implies exactions from an independent set of processes: that is, by "extortion." Extortion or exaction involves, as we have seen, no exchange. The value of the resources exacted cannot be fixed in relation to the productivity of the processes yielding resources offered in exchange. Hence, the value systems of the two sets of processes are disjoint. The means of production in the processes subject to exaction, the processes in the subordinate economy, are possessed by the agents operating those processes – both in the sense of this essay and in the sense of Marx. Each agent in the subordinate economy may have the right to exclude any other from the resources in his or her possession. Since the same processes may be subject to rights in property in a different (dominant) value system, the nominal owner under that system may have the right to exclude others in the same system from making exactions on the same set of processes. What is important, however, is that any relation between the agents in possession of the means of production in the subordinate enonomy and the agents making exactions on that economy is one of power – of politics or ideology. This is as true of the relation between dominant and subordinate human agents as it is of the relation between the agents of the human economies and the natural environment they exploit.

The other side of the coin is that so long as the agents in the subordinate economy respond to a distinct set of signals, then the control exercised by the agents of the dominant economy will be limited. It is this aspect of the relation between dominant and subordinate economies that has been the subject of such enduring concern in the development literature. The real problem identified in that literature is the uncontrollability of the production processes undertaken by people responding to a different set of signals altogether. Whether discussion hinges on the persistence of archaic attitudes to the accumulation of capital in Rostovian "pre-take-off" economies, or the role of politics and the state in colonial economies characterized by the articulation of modes of production, the point at issue is the inability of market signals to effect an allocation of resources that is efficient by the criteria of the dominant group in the society. Analogously, it is the uncontrollability of the processes of the environment in terms of the signals of the economy that is the biggest single problem facing those concerned with the management of the global system. What makes this interesting is that it turns out that the market solution does not directly address the control problem at all, resting as it does on the extraordinarily powerful assumption that property is sufficient to give control.

It is partly to lay the foundations for an assessment of the market solution that this chapter considers the problem of environmental control via the price mechanism.

6.2 External effects

Before proceeding any further, it is useful to situate the concepts described so far in terms of the conventional wisdom on the limits of the price system. More particularly, it is helpful to consider the current understanding of the causes and significance of effects that are unsignalled by the price system, the external effects. Recall that the basis for the existence of external effects in an economy-environment system is the unobservability of the general system through the signals of the economy, the price system. Where, for example, the disposal of wastes generated in the production of some economic good into the environment rebounds on some process or processes within the economy, but is not reflected in the price of that good, the effect is said to be external to the price system. So we have at the core of the definition of external effects the following: "an external effect arises wherever the value of a production function, or a consumption function, depends directly [not mediated by the price system] upon the activities of others" (Mishan, 1971, p. 3). On this there is little disagreement. Indeed, it accurately reflects the sense of Meade's interdependencies. To interpret this in terms of the arguments of this essay, however, we need to touch on an area in which there is much less agreement. According to Mishan, again, "the essential feature of the concept of an external effect is that it is not a deliberate creation but an unintended or incidental by-product of some otherwise legitimate activity" (1971, p. 3). The words "unintended" and "incidental" are, however, misleading. An effect that is not captured by the price mechanism implies only that it is not observable in terms of the price signals of the economy. It does not imply that the effect is either unintended by the agent or institution controlling the process, or that it is incidental to the process. The immediacy of the effects of some acts of pollution (noise pollution, for example) imply that they are fully "intended," but are nevertheless not reflected in the structure of relative prices. It may well be that particular effects are accidental, but this is not a necessary part of the definition of external effects. What is necessary is that the effects are not negotiated between the parties concerned.

It is this feature that Meade's (1973) definition seizes on: "An external economy (diseconomy) is an event which confers an appreciable benefit (inflicts an appreciable damage) on some person or persons who were not fully consenting parties in reaching the decision or decisions which led directly or indirectly to the event in question" (1973, p. 15). Although this definition is somewhat ambiguous, the link it implies between the existence of external effects and the exactions and insertions of matter on and into the environment should be clear. Since the concept of a transaction under the price system implies an exchange in which both parties share the gains from trade by agreement, external effects are necessarily associated with the force majeure of exactions and insertions.

We have already seen that the value system distinguishes between resources that may be observed via the price mechanism and those that may not. We have also seen that the zero-valuation of resources that are either inputs or outputs of the valorized processes implies a power relation between the agents controlling the positively and zero-valued resources. An *environmental external effect* may accordingly be defined as the change in the value of the outputs of a given economic process or processes resulting from a quantitative or qualitative change in the inputs exacted from the environment by the process(es) due to exactions on or insertions into the environment by the same or some other process(es). What is important is that since the processes of the environment are not valorized, the impact of the disposal of economic residuals in the environment, or the depletion of environmental resources, is not observable through the price system.

There are, then, two conditions required for the existence of environmental external effects. The first is technical, the second broadly social. The first is that the economy and its environment are in a relation of mutual dependence. this ensures that there are real exchanges between the processes of the economy and those of the environment; that the economy and its environment are jointly determined. The second is that the price system provides an incomplete set of measures of the physical system. Not all resources are observed in the process of commodity exchange. Markets are, in other words, incomplete. These are, in fact, both necessary and sufficient conditions. In any input indecomposable system, where the expansion of the economy depends on exaction or the exploitation of "natural" resources, and in which the free gifts and free disposals assumptions do not hold, there will exist environmental external effects. It is only if the disposal of residuals in the environment or the exploitation of environmental resources have no impact at all on the outputs of the environment, that they will not be associated with external effects. Hence the assumption of free gifts and free disposals is, at the same time, the assumption of zero environmental external effects.

Economically, the measure of environmental external effects is taken to be the "social" costs and benefits they involve. Although these may be defined in value terms, they are not derived from either private or public accounts. They are, as Kapp has pointed out, the "consequences of productive activities and policy decisions which, for several reasons, carry an inevitable residuum of indeterminacy but which are nevertheless real and important – even though their approximate magnitude can be determined only after careful factual study and which in many instances call for an evaluation based on criteria other than market values" (1969, p. 345). Social environmental costs or benefits are thus an indirect and very far from precise measure of the environmental impact of economic activities.

Technically, environmental external effects may arise if there is a change in the outputs of the processes of the environment either *quantitatively* or *qualitatively*. A qualitative change in the outputs of the environment implies a change in the coefficients of the rows of the gross input matrix describing the use made of environmental resources. So, by our earlier example, a process that ordinarily makes use of clean air would, in the event of the insertion of suspended compounds of sulphur into the air, be modified by the appearance of sulphur compounds into the list of its inputs. If, in consequence of this, there was a reduction in the value of the net output of that process, the disposal of sulphur compounds in the air may be said to have resulted in a negative external effect. If there was an increase in the value of its net output, then the external effect may be said to have been positive. Qualitative environmental external effects are ordinarily discussed as problems of pollution.

By contrast, a quantitative change in the outputs of the environment implies no change in the input coefficients of the processes of the economy and is not immediately reflected in a change in relative resource values. Nonetheless, by changing the point at which the viability condition becomes binding for a particular natural resource, it has a potential effect on future resource values. The erosion of potentially arable land not currently in cultivation, for example, has no immediate effect on relative prices, but by tightening the limits on the physical growth of the economy it affects the time path of future relative prices. Quantitative environmental external effects are ordinarily discussed as problems of resource depletion.

Recall that Meade (1952) distinguished between the direct interdependence of processes, which he argued to produce "unpaid factors of production," and the indirect interdependence of processes, which he argued to be responsible for the "creation of atmosphere." In the direct relationship the output of one activity is affected by the direct insertion of (unpriced) inputs to the activity deriving from some other activity. In the indirect relationship the output of one activity is affected by the state of an (unpriced) environment that is common to a number of activities and that is itself affected by one or more of those other activities.

This technical distinction between direct and indirect relations has since been used to develop a well-known "social" theory of external effects. The different prospects for generating markets in the resources directly responsible for external effects under the two sets of relations have encouraged a distinction between two types of external effect. Since Coase (1960), the direct relationship has been seen as a problem of incomplete markets for *private goods;* the incompleteness of the markets being explained by Dahlman (1979) and Demsetz (1967) to be a function of the level of transaction costs relative to the value of the external effect. It is argued to be susceptible of solution by the establishment of markets for the external effects through the allocation of property rights. The indirect relationship, on the other hand, represents a residual problem in the nonexclusiveness of public goods, and is argued to be susceptible to solution by either Pigouvian taxes/subsidies or by quantitative restrictions imposed on the producers of external effects (cf. Baumol, 1972, and Baumol and Oates, 1975, 1979). In other words, it is seen as a problem in the allocation of resources subject to common rights of property where these are defined to include all resources not subject to private property rights. Common property rights and the unrecognized (private) property rights referred to earlier are assumed to be the same thing.

6.3   Price and property

To explore the significance of property rights for the price system, we need to isolate the signals of the economy, the value system. The first step here is to distinguish between those processes subject to property rights and those that are not. To do this we may premultiply the technology matrices by the time-indexed diagonal selection matrix, $\mathbf{I}_{h(k)}$: that is the matrix with h of the n elements on the principal diagonal equal to one and all other elements equal to zero. $I_{h(k)}$ thus selects out the h processes in the global system subject to property rights. These include all those processes that generate economic goods. If $h(k) < h(k + 1)$ the number of processes subject to property rights is expanding, if $h(k) > h(k + 1)$, it is contracting. Recalling the definition of the economy as an informationally distinct subsystem, we see that $I_{h(k)}$ thus indicates the maximum dimensions of this subsystem. We may note, in passing, that there will be as many such selection matrices as there are informationally distinct subsystems, and wherever the sum of the indices of all selection matrices exceeds the number of rows in the technology matrices, there will be the multiple possession of resources referred to earlier.

The main implication of the introduction of $I_{h(k)}$ is that the price system will have, at most, h positive components. If the rows of the technology matrices are ordered such that the h processes subject to rights of property are listed first, the first h components of $\mathbf{p}(k)$ at most will be positive, the last $n - h$ components will all be zero. Similarly, $\mathbf{r}(k)$, the vector of process revenues, will be positive in the first h components at most. The two vectors are now related by the equation

$$\mathbf{r}(k + 1) = D\mathbf{q}(k)I_{h(k)}\mathbf{B}(k)\mathbf{p}(k + 1) \qquad 6.1$$

where $D\mathbf{q}(k) = \text{diagonal } [q_1, \ldots, q_n]$, yielding the fundamental price equations

$$I_{h(k)}\mathbf{B}(k)\mathbf{p}(k + 1) = I_{h(k)}\mathbf{A}(k)[I + D\mathbf{w}(k)]\mathbf{p}(k) \qquad 6.2$$

Written in full, these are of the form

$$
\begin{bmatrix}
1_1 & & & & \mathbf{0} \\
& \ddots & & & \\
& & 1_h & & \\
& & & 0_{h+1} & \\
& & & & \ddots \\
\mathbf{0} & & & & 0_n
\end{bmatrix}
$$

$$
\begin{bmatrix}
b_{11} \cdots b_{1h} \, 0 & \cdots 0 \\
\cdots\cdots\cdots\cdots\cdots\cdots\cdots \\
b_{h1} \cdots b_{hh} \, b_{hh+1} & \cdots \, b_{hn} \\
0 \cdots 0 \; b_{h+1h+1} \cdots b_{h+1n} \\
\cdots\cdots\cdots\cdots\cdots\cdots\cdots \\
0 \cdots 0 \; b_{nh+1} & \cdots \, b_{nn}
\end{bmatrix} (k)
\begin{bmatrix}
p_1 \\
\vdots \\
p_h \\
0 \\
\vdots \\
0
\end{bmatrix} (k + 1)
$$

$$6.3$$

$$
= \begin{bmatrix} 1_1 & & & \\ & \vdots & & \mathbf{0} \\ & 1_h & & \\ & & 0_{n+1} & \\ & & \vdots & \\ \mathbf{0} & & & 0_n \end{bmatrix} \begin{bmatrix} a_{11} & \cdots a_{1h} & a_{1h+1} & \cdots & a_{1n} \\ \cdots\cdots\cdots\cdots\cdots\cdots\cdots\cdots \\ a_{h1} & \cdots a_{hh} & a_{hh+1} & \cdots & a_{hn} \\ a_{h+11} & \cdots a_{h+1h} & a_{h+1h+1} & \cdots & a_{h+1h} \\ \cdots\cdots\cdots\cdots\cdots\cdots\cdots\cdots \\ a_{n1} & \cdots a_{nh} & a_{nh+1} & \cdots & a_{nn} \end{bmatrix} (k)
$$

$$
\begin{bmatrix} 1+w_1 & & & \\ & \vdots & & \mathbf{0} \\ & 1+w_h & & \\ & & 0_{n+1} & \\ \mathbf{0} & & & \vdots \\ & & & 0_n \end{bmatrix} (k) \begin{bmatrix} p_1 \\ \vdots \\ p_h \\ 0 \\ \vdots \\ 0 \end{bmatrix} (k)
$$

The first h columns in the first h rows of $\mathbf{A}(k)$ and $\mathbf{B}(k)$ describe the inputs to and outputs from the processes subject to property rights. The columns $h + 1$ to n in the last $n - h$ rows of $\mathbf{A}(k)$ describe the insertions (exactions) of the products of such processes in (by) the environmental processes. The last $n - h$ columns in the first h rows of $\mathbf{A}(k)$ describe the exactions (insertions) of the products of environmental processes by (in) the proprietory processes. Notice, though, that $p_i(k) \geq 0$ for $i \in \{1, \ldots ,h\}$. The first h prices are not necessarily positive. $p_i(k) > 0$ only if the ith element on the principal diagonal of $\mathbf{I}_{h(k)} = 1$, but proprietory rights in the ith process are not sufficient to ensure that $p_i(k) > 0$. In fact $p_i(k) > 0$ for all $i \in \{1, \ldots ,h\}$ if and only if $\mathbf{I}_{h(k)}$ is positive in the first h elements on the principal diagonal, *and* $a_{ij}(k) > 0$ for at least one j and for all $i \in \{1, \ldots ,h\}$. If $a_{ij}(k) = 0$ for all $j \in \{1, \ldots ,h\}$ we have property without possession, and $p_i(k) = 0$.

Zero prices in the system convey no information on the corresponding resources beyond the fact that under the prevailing system of property rights (and in the current period) they are nonscarce. They ensure that the system is not completely observable through the set of prices. In such circumstances, the allocation of resources in a dynamic system subject to the conservation of mass on the basis of the prices of positively valued resources only will have a range of unanticipated indirect external effects. The implication of the relation between property, possession, and price just discussed is that this problem will not disappear with the allocation of rights of property in environmental processes.

To see this at a strictly microeconomic level, notice that we can describe the production function for the ith economic process in the system using the input and output vectors (since the function is linearly homogeneous)

$$b_i(k) = h[a_i(k)] \qquad\qquad 6.4$$

Since $a_i(\mathrm{k})$ is an n-dimensional vector, it includes both economic and environmental inputs. More particularly, there are $n - h$ inputs representing exactions on the environment. These are zero priced and so unobserved through the economy. Analogously, $b_i(k)$ lists both economic and noneconomic outputs. The former are a function both of current economic inputs and the external environmental effects caused by the past behavior of the agents of the system. To reflect the historic environmental effects of economic activity, we may write

$$[b_{i1}(k), \ldots, b_{ih}(k)] = f[a_{i1}(k), \ldots, a_{ih}(k)]g[\mathbf{q}(k - t,k)] \qquad 6.5$$

where $g[\mathbf{q}(k - t,k)]$ describes the impact on the productivity of the economic inputs in the ith process of the (external) effects of allocations made over the interval $(k - t,k)$. These effects work through the economically unobserved environmental inputs to the ith process, $[a_{ih+1}(k), \ldots, a_{in}(k)]$, and are assumed to scale the output obtainable from a given set of economic inputs. The length of the interval $(k - t,k)$ will depend on the length of the chain connecting the processes of the economy. In all cases, though, a change in the elements $a_{ij}(k - t)b_{ij}(k - t)$ for $i \in \{h + 1, \ldots, n\}$, $t > 0$, as a result of either waste disposal in the last $n - h$ processes or depletion of the last $n - h$ resources, will involve effects on the elements $a_{ij}(k)b_{ij}(k)$ for $j \in \{h + 1, \ldots, n\}$ that will not be registered in the price system. The marginal social costs or benefits of the level of activity in the ith process in the $(k - t)$th period will then be given by the first partial derivative of the function $g[\mathbf{q}(k - t,k)]$ with respect to $q_i(k - t)$, $g_i(k - t)$. If less than zero, it implies a negative external effect; if greater than zero it implies a positive external effect. A negative external effect implies that a marginal increase in the mass of resources advanced in the processes of the economy will reduce the economically valued output obtainable from a given set of economically valued inputs. A positive external effect increases the output obtainable.

Consider a typically simplified example. Let the nth (environmental) resource be subject to no well-defined property rights, and let it be employed with the jth (economic) product in the production of the ith (economic) product. The ex-post demands made on the resource in the kth period are given by $\mathbf{q}(k)a_n(k)$. Output of the ith product in the kth period, $q_i(k + 1)$, is given by $\mathbf{q}(k)\mathbf{b}_i(k)$, in which

$$b_{ii}(k) = f[a_{ij}(k)]g[\mathbf{q}(k)\mathbf{a}_n(k)] \qquad\qquad 6.6$$

where $g_j < 0$ if $q_n(k) \leq \mathbf{q}(k)\mathbf{a}_n(k)$, and $g_j = 0$ if $q_n(k) > \mathbf{q}(k)\mathbf{a}_n(k)$, $j = 1, \ldots, n - 1$. In other words, the average output of the ith product is a decreasing function of the level of activity of all users of the nth resource wherever stocks of the nth resource are at or below a threshold level (reflecting, say, the biotic potential of the resource). In these circumstances an increase in the level of activity in any one process using the nth resource imposes a negative external effect on all producers of the ith product in the form of reduced average yields of that product.

If the nth resource is exploited competitively, then the optimal level of activity in the ith process will be given by choice of $q_i(k)$ to maximize

$$q_i(k)f[a_{ij}(k)]p_i(k + 1)g[\mathbf{q}(k)\mathbf{a}_n(k)] - q_i(k)a_{ij}(k)p_j(k) \qquad 6.7$$

subject to

$$1 - \sum_j q_i(k)a_{jn}(k)/q_n(k) \geq a_{nn}(k) \qquad j = 1, \ldots, n - 1 \qquad 6.8$$

It may be readily checked that for 6.7 to be at a maximum with the constraints binding

$$f[a_{ij}(k)]p_i(k + 1)g[\mathbf{q}(k)\mathbf{a}_n(k)] + q_i(k)f[a_{ij}(k)]p_i(k + 1)g_i$$
$$= a_{ij}(k)p_j(k) - \mu_i a_{in}(k)/q_n(k) \qquad 6.9$$

in which μ_i is a measure of the user cost of the quantity of the nth resource required in the ith process at the chosen level of activity.

It has been argued since Gordon (1954) that where the resource is exploited by many agents, each with guaranteed rights of access to it, then the user cost of the resource will be ignored by each agent. It then follows that the optimal level of exploitation of the resource by many competitive agents will be higher than the optimal level of exploitation of a similar private resource by a single agent. Hence, it is claimed that common property in the resources of the environment encourage their overexploitation. Now the user cost of a resource will obviously be ignored if $p_n(k)$, $w_n(k)$ and the nth element on the principal diagonal of $\mathbf{I}_{h(k)}$ are all zero – which is the case when the nth resource is subject to no well-defined rights of property. Notice, though, that this is not the same thing as saying that the resource is in common property. There is a very important distinction to be drawn between common property subject to regulated use, *res publicus,* and open access property, *res nullius* (see Repetto and Holmes, 1983, and the earlier work of Ciriacy-Wantrup, 1952). There is no difficulty in finding historical evidence to support the hypothesis that open access resources tend to be exploited in a profligate manner, but not all resources in the public domain have been subject to open access, nor have they all been over-exploited. Indeed, common property resources subject to controlled access have tended to be underexploited by the criteria of private agents. We will return to this distinction later. What is immediately interesting, though, is not that controlled access common property resources exist, but that open access resources are overexploited because the user costs are unrecorded in the price system.

6.4   The price system and the limits of control

Now consider the systemic problem. We can easily see that the zero-pricing of environmental resources is sufficient to ensure the uncontrollability of the general system. First, let us partition the technology matrices $A(k)$ and $B(k)$ as in 6.3.

$$A(k) = \begin{bmatrix} A_{11} & A_{12} \\ A_{21} & A_{22} \end{bmatrix} (k) \qquad 6.10$$

The h processes described by the row $\underline{A}_1(k)$ describe the economy, and the $n - h$ processes described by the row $\underline{A}_2(k)$ describes its environment. $A_{21}(k)$ describes the insertion of economic wastes in the environment (pollution). $A_{12}(k)$ describes the exaction of raw materials from the environment (depletion).

$$B(k) = \begin{bmatrix} B_{11} & 0 \\ 0 & B_{23} \end{bmatrix} (k) \qquad 6.11$$

$B_{11}(k)$ and $B_{22}(k)$ describe the outputs of economic and environmental processes, respectively. The price vector, $p(k)$, is semipositive, having at most h positive components. The last $n - h$ outputs are zero valued.

The limitations of price signals as observers of the general system in this case (where $A(k)$ is indecomposable) may again be illustrated by reference to the control problem. Recall that the state space representation of the time-variant physical system is

$$q(k + 1) = q(k)B(k - 1) + j(k)M(k) \qquad 6.12$$

where $j(k) = q(k)[I - A(k - 1)]$ is the vector of control variables. Now if we describe the processes of the economy alone, where $q(k)$, $j(k)$ and $M(k)$ are partitioned conformably with the partitioning of $A(k)$ and $B(k)$ in 6.10 and 6.11, then 6.12 is of the form

$$q_1(k + 1) = q_1(k)B_{11}(k - 1) + j_1(k)M(k) \qquad 6.13$$

with $j_1(k) = q_1(k)[I - A_{11}(k - 1)]$. The state variables of the control system are the components of the vector $q_1(k)$, and are regulated through the application of the residuals generated in the economy – the difference between the resources available to the system at the beginning of the kth period and those required under the technology inherited from the $k - 1$th period, $q_1(k)[I - A_{11}(k - 1)]$.

The "outputs" of this system, in a control sense, are the resource prices in 6.8, and not the residuals themselves (which are the control system "outputs" under a system of control by stock levels). The prices of the resources produced in the economy inform the allocation of resources. These measures are, of course, rather more complex than the simple residuals in a system of control by stock levels, since they record both the relative productivity of the processes of the economy and the impact on the distributive variables of the relative market (and political) power of the different classes of proprietor. The two sets of measures are not equivalent. What they do have in common, however, is that both are of the same dimension as the economy. That is, both the vector of residuals and the price system are described by h dimensional vectors. Under both sets of measures the general system is observable in respect of the first h processes only, and in respect of the first h resources employed in the first h processes. The price system, like the vector of economic residuals, conveys no information about the output of resources in the nonvalorized system – the nonscarce resources exacted from the environment. It follows, by reasoning analogous to that in 4.3 and 4.4, that just as the agents operating the processes of the valorized system will not be able to observe the outputs of the environment, so they will not be able to control the production of resources in the environment.

If the general system were input decomposable, so that the economy made no insertions into its environment, the unobservability of the environment through the price signals of the economy would mean only that the agents of the economy would be unable to "see" the impending scarcity of any of the resources exacted from the environment. It would only be when the exacted resources begin to disappear and force some intervention in their production that the price system would be called upon to force an adjustment in the economy. Since the global system is not generally decomposable, the implications of the unobservability of the environment are more serious. Any change in the technology governing the material transformations of the economy will have an effect on the structure and volume of the wastes generated by the economy. If these are disposed of within the environment, it follows that there will be a range of effects that cannot be anticipated from a reading of the price signals of the economy. Only if these effects subsequently influence either the quantity or quality of natural resources available to the economy will they be noticed.

6.5   Property, possession, and control reconsidered

To return to the matters discussed in Section 6.1, we are now in a position to decide on the merits of the allocation of property rights as a solution to the problem of external effects. The matter is important precisely because it lies at the core of the market solution to the problem, under which the allocation of appropriate private property rights among the parties to an external effect is argued to be sufficient to ensure an efficient solution in most cases of interest. Dasgupta and Heal are particularly eminent proponents of this view. They argue, for example, that problems associated with common or communal property of arable or grazing land can be solved "at one stroke" by the simple act of legislating property rights (1979; p. 77). Similarly confident pronouncements are to be found everywhere in the literature.

Once we clarify the distinction between property and possession, however, it is easy to see the fundamental flaw in the simple logic of the problem of the common. The allocation of rights in property over a resource is a necessary but not a sufficient condition for the generation of prices which, at equilibrium, will reflect its relative scarcity. Since the positive pricing of a resource implies that positively valued inputs are advanced in its production, property without possession provides no basis for the generation of prices. For the user cost of a resource to be more than an arbitrary private royalty, a claim on the social surplus, it is necessary for the output of that resource to be controlled in some measure through the management of its inputs. So long as this does not happen the general system will be neither observable nor controllable. All prices will be subject to Kapp's "residuum of indeterminacy." Where property is not accompanied by possession such a residuum becomes infinitely large.

This has not stopped some from pushing the logic of the common as far as it will go. It is, for example, a Coaseian logic that has prompted at least one writer to discuss the environment in terms of the concept of biological capital, in which "unharvested resources" or "living biological capital" is priced like any product of the processes of the economy (Smith, 1977). Few other ideas in economic theory can be so obviously misplaced. It is one thing to haggle, ex post, over more or less obvious external effects realized more or less immediately. It is another thing entirely to pretend that property alone would enable all effects to be anticipated in the normal transactions between the human proprietors of the system. Indeed, the last idea represents a logic akin to that which moved mediaeval pontiffs to "solve" the problems of the spiritual world by allocating property in vast uncharted areas of the globe to one or other holy order. Property in a resource is simply not sufficient to generate an appropriate measure of its scarcity.

In fact, the practical difficulties in identifying property rights are alone sufficient to preclude the privatization of the global resources. Dasgupta and Heal, in less bullish frame of mind, recognize this. In their own entertaining mixture of metaphors "to search for Nirvana via competitive markets is rather like searching for the Holy Grail. An entire class of potential property markets for externality may fail to develop simply because of the difficulty in establishing property rights" (1979, p. 51). However, even if property rights can be established, they will fail to generate an adequate set of signals unless accompanied by possession. What matters is control, not title.

CHAPTER 7

Economic conflict and environmental change

7.1   Conflict and change: an historical perspective

The powerful sweep of history, more than anything else, is what distinguishes the works of the classical political economists from the post-Walrasian literature. Walsh and Gram (1980) have, as we have seen, described this as a difference of theme; the theme of the former being "the capacity of an economy to reproduce itself and grow," that of the latter being "the allocation of given resources." The contrast between the dynamic approach of one and the static approach of the other is certainly striking. O'Brien (1975) has commented on the irony that something taken so much for granted by the classical political economists could have disappeared so completely in the wake of the marginalist revolution of the 1870s. Although the thematic distinction captures the difference between the dynamic general equilibrium models of the Neumann type and those with a Walrasian basis, however, it fails to reach the classical political economists' obsession with the driving forces of change in the economic system. For even though the dynamic general equilibrium models are satisfied by the introduction of mechanical "time" into a fixed-technology world, the classical political economists were after something much more significant. They were fascinated by the source of the restless change they observed in the capitalist economy – not a mechanical clockwork measure of the rhythms of the economy. Indeed, Marx spent a lifetime trying to uncover the "laws of motion" of a system that was and still is constantly regenerating itself by adopting new guises.

The notion that societal or systemic change is the product of internal tensions or contradictions, although implicit in many works of classical political economy, is now associated with Marx. In Marx's work it received a sharper focus and more rigorous philosophical underpinning than in any previous contribution. Its outlines are familiar enough to require no more than a cursory review. Spelled out in the chapter on the Historical Tendency of Capitalist Accumulation in *Capital I* (Marx, 1954) and the 1959 Preface to the *Contribution to the Critique of Political Economy* (Marx, 1971), the argument holds that

95

the emergence of contradictions between the forces and relations of production in given societies explains their mutation. The structure of society was argued by Marx to be given by these relations of production, with each set of relations based on a corresponding set of property rights. If, at any stage in its history, the material productive forces of a society – its technology and resource base – became inconsistent with the demands associated with the prevailing relations of production, the resulting contradiction could only be resolved by changing the corresponding set of property rights. Marx argued that since the emergence of such contradictions was inherent in the development of the forces of production, so too was the social revolution implied by their resolution.

What is interesting for our purposes is that the emergence of a contradiction of this sort is argued to be registered in class conflict, which in turn implies a distributional contest over the spoils of environmental exploitation. To get a feeling for this at a lower level of abstraction it is worth considering Marx's comments in the introduction to the *Grundrisse* (1973). Here he was concerned with establishing the interrelatedness of change at the level of both production and distribution. He pointed out that "all production is appropriation of nature on the part of an individual within and through a specific form of society. In this sense it is a tautology to say that property (appropriation) is a precondition of production" (1973, p. 87). All economic production implies a particular set of property rights carrying with them a particular set of entitlements to the social product. But it is clear that unlike Walras he did not take the distribution of assets to be a given datum. Nor did he suppose that the form of production was independent of the nature and distribution of property rights. Indeed, he pointed to the existence of numerous historical examples in which a change in the distribution of entitlements through a change in the distribution of assets caused a change in the form of production:

As regards whole societies, distribution seems to precede production and to determine it in yet another respect, almost as if it were a pre-economic fact. A conquering people divides the land among the conquerors, thus imposes a certain distribution and form of property in land, and thus determines production. Or it enslaves the conquered and so makes slave labour the foundation of production. Or a people rises in revolution and smashes the great landed estates into small parcels, and hence, by this new distribution, gives production a new character. Or a system of law assigns property in land to certain families in perpetuity, or distributes labour as a hereditary privilege and thus confines it within certain castes. In all these cases, and they are all historical, it seems that distribution is not structured and determined by production, but rather the opposite, production by distribution (1973, p. 96).

It is worth noting, in passing, the stark contrast between this and the inference to be drawn from the unbiasedness property of competitive equilibrium in the Walrasian system. Recall that this property states that the efficiency of the outcome in a competitive exchange economy will not be compromised by any change in the distribution of assets. A Pareto optimal solution associated with a given set of preferences and techniques of production will be attainable for any distribution of assets. The inference is that the form, the organization, and the technology of production are independent of the distribution of assets. Against this Marx claimed that a change in the distribution of assets is in fact sufficient to induce a change in the conditions of production. Elsewhere, Marx was at pains to argue that the treatment of distribution independently of production was illusory, and that ultimately it was the conditions of production and not the conditions of distribution that dominated. But in this and similar passages (cf. 1973, pp. 99–100) he drew attention to the fact that at particular moments in history one of the main sources of change in the conditions of production was conflict over the distribution either of property rights in assets (economic resources) or the entitlements of those with such rights. A distributional contest has historically been sufficient to bring about technological change.

Methodologically, this implies that while the various moments of the economic process – production, distribution, exchange, consumption – are to be regarded as the interdependent parts of an "organic whole" existing in historical time, it is possible to isolate the effects of a change in one element at one moment in time. We have tended to think that a partial approach so similar to the comparative statics of later equilibrium analysis was to be found in Ricardo, but not in Marx. It does, however, seem clear that Marx was aware that the act of taking a slice out of the historical process separates the resulting segment of time from its "historical environment." Moreover, even though he did not regard such segments of time as independent of their historical environment, he was ready to explore them for evidence of the laws of motion of the organic whole.

Recall, from Section 5.3, that it is the property of the sociotechnological matrix $\mathbf{B}^{-1}\mathbf{A}[\mathbf{I} + \mathbf{Dw}]$ and not the technology matrix $\mathbf{B}^{-1}\mathbf{A}$ that is of interest in looking at the time behavior of the price system of an economy subject to distributional conflict. In this chapter I explore the general impact of a distributional contest between economic agents in an economy-environment system within a similarly (temporally) partial framework. To isolate the effects of a change in the distribution of income as opposed to a change in the distribution of assets, however,

I make the conventional assumption that the distribution of assets does not change in the time segment under scrutiny. This discussion is not intended to offer a characterization of the general process of historical change but merely to indicate the logical basis of the connection between conflict and the environmental and economic change explored in this essay.

The interest of the time effects of a distributional contest lies in its implications for the Coase solution to the problem of external effects. Although the following analysis enables us to verify the intuitive short-period result that any tax on a polluter should reduce the immediate level of pollution, it suggests that the long-period effects will be much less clear. Any redistribution of income implies an alteration in the raw materials of change, the residuals of the system.

7.2   Economic residuals: economic waste and investment

We have seen that the existence of external effects in an economy-environment system is a function of either exactions on or insertions into the processes of the environment. The first implies the depletion of environmental resources, the second involves the pollution of environmental processes. Where economy and environment are mutually dependent, exactions or insertions by one sector on or into the other will necessarily rebound. We have also seen that the residuals generated in the economy may be applied either to the processes of the economy as investment, or to the processes of the environment as waste. It does not necessarily follow, therefore, that high levels of residuals imply high rates of investment. They may equally imply high rates of pollution. To explore this we need first to clarify the distinction between waste and investment, and between economic and noneconomic waste.

The negative of the vector of excess demands, defined in 5.11 for the technologically stationary case, is the vector of residuals, $q_R(k)$, defined here for the time-variant case:

$$q_R(k) = q(k)[I - A(k - 1)] \qquad 7.1$$

This vector includes all those resources – investment, economic, and noneconomic waste – not required for production under the inherited technology. In Part I we saw that, under the conservation of mass condition, the existence of residuals in the inherited technology will force some adjustment in the current technology of the system since, ex post, $q(k)[I - A(k)] = 0$ for all $k \geq 0$. This is, in fact, the *fons et origo* of technological change in the general system. Of course, if we operate with the powerful environmental assumption of free disposals, then the system is no longer required to adjust to the presence of residuals. That is, if the sequence $\{\mathbf{q}(k)\}$ is convergent, then so long as we make the assumption of free disposals, $\lim_{k\to\infty}\mathbf{q}(k)[\mathbf{I} - \mathbf{A}(k)] \geq 0$ is quite compatible with the case where $\mathbf{A}(k) = \mathbf{A}(0)$ for all $k > 0$. In other words, under the free disposals assumption, the existence of positive residuals is quite compatible with the time invariance or technological stationarity of the system. In a closed economy-environment system where the conservation of mass condition holds, however, free disposal fails.

As a first step we may identify the economic residuals generated in a jointly determined economy-environment system. Let the general system be partitioned as in 6.10 and 6.11. We can then identify a nonzero vector $\mathbf{q}_1(k)[\mathbf{I} - \mathbf{A}_{11}(k)]$, whose positive components represent resources that, though products of the economy, are surplus to the requirements of the economy under the technology applied in the kth period. They are unemployed in the economy in that period. They thus represent economic waste and so, by implication, indicate the existence of excess capacity in the economy.

Note that this set of products includes those waste products for which there is no known potential economic use and so no economic value, such as the effluent of industry. As we saw in Chapter 6 it is not implied that all outputs of the first h processes are necessarily positively valued. The disposal of these noneconomic wastes is recorded in the rows of $\mathbf{A}_{12}(k)$.

The wasted part of an economic product may accordingly be defined as the quantity of the residual of that product which is not reinvested in the processes of the economy. All resources that are unemployed in this sense will of course go somewhere: that is, they will be disposed of in some sort of activity. The meaning of free disposal in such a context would be that such disposals could have no effect on the future elements of $\mathbf{A}_{11}(k + h)$ and $\mathbf{B}_{11}(k + h)$, $h = 1,2,\ldots$ Residuals not required in the processes of the economy could be costlessly disposed of in the environment within which the economy operates. Their disposal would involve no external effects. Since, as we have already seen, the free disposal of residuals implies the physical independence of the economy from its environment, and since this has been ruled out, the disposal of waste products is not free. All disposals carry the potential for future external effects.

As a first approximation the unemployed or wasted portion of the h

resources produced in the economy in the $k - 1$th period may be
defined by

$$\mathbf{q}_{R1}(k)\mathbf{Du}(k) = \mathbf{q}_{R1}(k)[\mathbf{I} - \mathbf{Dv}(k)\mathbf{A}_{11}(k)] \qquad 7.2$$

where $u_i(k)$, $v_i(k)$ in the diagonal, h-square, matrices $\mathbf{Du}(k)$ and $\mathbf{Dv}(k)$
denote the proportion of the residual of the ith product which is,
respectively, unemployed in the processes of the economy or is dedicated for investment. The rate of unemployment of resources or economic waste is thus a function of both the technology of the economy
and the structure and level of investment. By the same token, the existence of external effects in the economy (from this source) is a function
of both the "technology" of the environment and the structure and
level of unemployment. We may accordingly get some indication of
the external effects of a distributional contest within the economy by
inquiring into the effect of changes in the returns to economic
resources on the level of their unemployment within the economy.

7.3   Economic conflict and the generation of waste

The immediate cause of the existence of waste among economic
resources is, by definition, a difference between the relative quantities
of economic resources produced within the system, and the requirements of the economy under a given technology and a given set of
activity levels. All wasted resources are, in this very general sense,
indicative of technological unemployment. That is, the unemployment
associated with a particular set of resources will vary with the technology applied in the economy. The waste or unemployment of human
resources – what the classical political economists called relative surplus population – is no different in this respect from the waste or
unemployment of any other product of the economy.

To repeat, the requirements of an economy for its own products are
a function of both the general technology applied in all processes in
that period and the level of activity of each process. The general technology determines the demand for each resource both directly (in the
processes employing the resource) and indirectly (in the processes
employing the outputs of the processes employing the resource) for a
given structure of activity levels. In a nonautomatous system where
the agents of the economy are able to withhold or advance resources
according to the signals of the system, the level of activity of each process is a function of the quantity of resources advanced for production.
More particularly, where the prices of resources are affected by the

level of excess demand via the distributive variables, then the level of activity of the process(es) yielding the ith resource will rise or fall with $w_i(k)$. Since the distributive variables are also affected by extra-economic (political, legal, or cultural factors) the level of activity of the processes of the economy will similarly reflect these factors. We may consider, therefore, the impact of such factors on the existence of economic waste.

To simplify the discussion I make several more or less restrictive assumptions. First, I assume that any investments made in the processes of the economy are extensive and not intensive. In other words, I assume that in the segment of the history of the system under examination the economy is technologically stationary, and that the act of investment has the effect of changing only the level of inputs advanced in and outputs yielded by the processes of the economy. This enables us to see the impact of extra-economic effects on the activity levels that fix the demand for resources in the economy for a given technology.

In general, of course, the technology of the economy is itself determined by extra-economic factors. The capacity for a system to adapt the technology rather than the level of activity of the economy when the signals of the system change is institutionally prescribed. Indeed, as we will see later, the thrust of much of the anthropological work on economies that are relatively stationary technologically suggests that it is the social institutions regulating those economies that prevents them from challenging the environmental constraints to growth by technological change. Since the regulation of activity levels is at least a short-period response to change in the signals of all systems, however, (compare the inventory cycle in modern capitalist economies) and since I am interested in the short-period effects of extra-economic influences, this seems to be a reasonable assumption.

In the time-variant (technologically dynamic) case the price system of the h dimensional economy described in 6.10 and 6.11 is of the form

$$Dq_1(k)B_{11}(k)p(k + 1) = [Dq_1(k)A_{11}(k - 1)$$
$$+ Dq_{R1}(k)Dv(k)A_{\Delta 11}(k - 1)][I + Dw(k)]p(k) \qquad 7.3$$

where all variables are as defined above. The matrix $Dq_{R1}(k)Dv(k)A_{\Delta 11}(k - 1) \leq Dq_{R1}(k)$ indicates the allocation of economic residuals, under the technology inherited from the $k - 1$th period, to the processes of the economy. The technological changes involved are described by the pair $A_{\Delta 11}(k - 1)$, $B_{\Delta 11}(k - 1)$. The diagonal matrix $Dq_{R1}(k)Dv(k)$ indicates the proportion of these residuals that is advanced for production or offered for employment. The effect of the assumption that the system is technologically stationary is that 7.3 simplifies to

$$Dq_1(k)B_{11}p(k+1)$$
$$= D[q_1(k) + q_{R1}(k)Dv(k)]A_{11}[I + Dw(k)]p(k) \quad 7.4$$

This has the advantage of making the analysis easier without qualitatively affecting the results. In addition, for ease of exposition, I assume that there is simple production: the ith resource is produced only by the ith process. The effect of this is that $Dq_1(k)B_{11}p(k+1)$ on the left-hand side of 7.4 may be written as $Dq_1(k+1)p(k+1)$. If we assume joint production, then 7.4 may be premultiplied by the inverse of $Dq_1(k-1)$; and the quantity vector on the right-hand side accordingly replaced by a vector indicating the rate of change in the quantity of inputs offered for employment.

The price system now has the form

$$Dq_1(k+1)p(k+1)$$
$$= [Dq_1(k) + Dq_{R1}(k)Dv(k)]A_{11}[I + Dw(k)]p(k) \quad 7.5$$

I now add the equivalent of the conventional identity between income and the sum of investment and consumption. This identity takes the form of a requirement that the total value of economic residuals in any one period, the value both of residuals dedicated for investment and destined to be wasted, is equal to the total income of all agents in the previous period. This implies that

$$q_{R1}(k+1)p(k+1)$$
$$= [q_1(k) + q_{R1}(k)Dv(k)]A_{11}Dw(k)p(k) \quad 7.6$$

It should be obvious that the first approximation of economic waste given in 7.2 in fact includes what is conventionally termed luxury consumption (the allocation of residuals in excess of the requirements of the economy under the inherited technology and preference system). In terms of this essay, 7.6 states that income in the kth period equals the sum of the value of waste and investment expenditure in the $k + 1$th period. We pay for the resources we produce but do not need.

We may now obtain an expression for the wasted resources of the economy in terms of the distributive variables fixed extra-economically. From 7.2 we have

$$q_{R1}(k+1)Du(k+1)p(k+1)$$
$$= q_{R1}(k+1)[I - Dv(k+1)A_{11}]p(k+1) \quad 7.7$$

Substituting 7.6 into 7.7 gives

$$\mathbf{q}_{R1}(k+1)\mathbf{Du}(k+1)\mathbf{p}(k+1) = [\mathbf{q}_1(k) + \mathbf{q}_{R1}(k)\mathbf{Dv}(k)]\mathbf{A}_{11}\mathbf{Dw}(k)\mathbf{p}(k)$$
$$- \mathbf{q}_{R1}(k+1)\mathbf{Dv}(k+1)\mathbf{A}_{11}\mathbf{p}(k+1)$$

7.8

Hence, for the ith resource:

$$q_{Ri}(k+1)u_i(k+1)p_i(k+1) = [\mathbf{q}_1(k) + \mathbf{q}_{R1}(k)\mathbf{Dv}(k)]\mathbf{a}_i w_i(k)p_i(k)$$
$$- \mathbf{q}_{R1}(k+1)\mathbf{Dv}(k+1)\mathbf{a}_i p_i(k+1)$$

7.9

$i \in \{1, \dots, h\}$. Substituting the ith equation from 7.5 into 7.9 yields, after manipulation,

$$\frac{q_{Ri}(k+1)u_i(k+1)}{q(k+1)} = \frac{[\mathbf{q}_1(k) + \mathbf{q}_{R1}(k)\mathbf{Dv}(k)]\mathbf{a}_i w_i(k)p_i(k)}{[q_i(k) + q_{Ri}(k)v_i(k)]\underline{\mathbf{a}}_i[\mathbf{I} + \mathbf{Dw}(k)]\mathbf{p}(k)}$$
$$- \frac{q_{R1}(k+1)\mathbf{Dv}(k+1)\mathbf{a}_i}{q_i(k+1)}$$

7.10

7.10 describes the rate of waste or unemployment of the ith resource produced by the economy in the $k + 1$th period in terms of the difference between two ratios. The first is the ratio of the income accruing to the proprietor or class of proprietors of the ith resource to the value of the output of the ith process in the kth period. The second is the rate of investment of the ith resource in the $k + 1$th period. Using this expression, we can explore the effect on the waste of any resource of political changes in the distribution of income to the proprietors of that resource.

7.4 Economic waste and environmental change

Consider the short-period effects on the rate of unemployment of the ith resource of a change in the rate of return on either ith resource. More particularly, consider the effects of a politically (exogenously) imposed change in the distributive variables in the kth period on the rate of unemployment or waste generation in the $k + 1$th period, holding the level of investment in the $k + 1$th period constant. Let us define the rate of unemployment of the ith resource in the $k + 1$th period as

$$u_i^*(k+1) = [q_{Ri}(k+1)u_i(k+1)]/q_i(k+1)$$

7.11

Then from 7.10 we have

$$du_i^*(k + 1)/dw_i(k) = (\{[q_i(k) + q_{Ri}(k)v_i(k)]\underline{a}_i[I + Dw(k)]p(k)\}$$
$$\{[\mathbf{q}_1(k) + \mathbf{q}_{R1}(k)Dv(k)]a_ip(k)\}$$
$$- \{[\mathbf{q}_1(k) + \mathbf{q}_{R1}(k)Dv(k)]a_iw_i(k)p_i(k)\}$$
$$\{[q_i(k) + q_{Ri}(k)v_i(k)]a_{ii}p_i(k)\})$$
$$\div [q_i(k) + q_{Ri}(k)v_i(k)]\underline{a}_i[I + Dw(k)]p(k)\}^2$$

7.12

An increase in the return on the ith resource will have the effect of causing unemployment of the ith resource to rise since, from the numerator of the right-hand side of 7.12

$$[q_i(k) + q_{Ri}(k)v_i(k)]a_{ii}w_i(k)p_i(k)$$
$$< [q_i(k) + q_{Ri}(k)v_i(k)]\underline{a}_i[I + Dw(k)]p(k + 1)   7.13$$

If the return to the proprietors of a particular resource is increased for noneconomic reasons, the proportion of that resource left idle or disposed of as waste within the general system will rise. To see the environmental effects of this perfectly intuitive result, recall that we have assumed that the technology of the economy does not, in the short period, react to the change in the distribution of income. It follows, therefore, that an increase in the economic residuals generated in a closed economy-environment system necessarily implies a change in the elements of the submatrices describing the environment. In other words, having ruled out the prospect of a substantive change in Marx's mode of economic production by assumption, at least in the short period, we are left with the necessity for substantive change in the nature of the processes of the environment. The logic is simple and direct. Since, ex post, $q_i(k) = q(k)a_i(k)$, for all $i \in \{1, \ldots, n\}$, and for all $k \geq 0$, it follows that $\mathbf{q}_1(k) = [\mathbf{q}_1(k) + \mathbf{q}_{R1}(k)Dv(k)]A_{11}(k) + q_{R2}(k)A_{21}(k)$. Assuming that $A_{21}(k - 1) = 0$, if $\mathbf{q}_1(k) > [\mathbf{q}_1(k) + q_{R1}(k)Dv(k)]A_{11}(k - 1)$, and if $A_{11}(k) = A_{11}(k - 1)$, then $A_{21}(k) \neq A_{21}(k - 1)$ and there exists at least one $a_{ij}(k) \in A_{21}(k) > 0$, $i = h+1, \ldots, n$.

A change in the distribution of income, or the entitlements of economic agents under a given set of property rights, will result in increased insertions into the environment: pollution. In Part I it was shown that a change in the inputs to a process will necessarily be reflected in change in the outputs of that process, hence these insertions will result in changes in the outputs of the processes of the environment. If the outputs of the environment are subject to exaction by the agents of the economy, and if the changes in the outputs of the environment affect the value of the outputs of the economic processes in which they are employed, then the original insertions will have generated economically unobserved (and therefore external) effects.

As noted earlier, the time taken for the realization of these effects is a function of the length of the chain connecting the valorized processes on either end of the externality. Hence, their relevance to the decision-making process is a function of the time horizon of the agents concerned. So the disposal of surplus radioactive materials on the sea bed reflects the fond belief of the agents concerned that even if the containers do fail, they will be protected for as long as matters by the length of the chain between the environmental processes immediately subject to radiation and the processes of the economy.

There is no difference here between economic and noneconomic wastes, the zero-valued effluent of economic activities. The latter will rise or fall with the level of activity, and so with the level of investment in exactly the same way as the former. Nor is the level of noneconomic wastes unaffected by changes in income distribution. Indeed, the inclusion of noneconomic wastes strengthens the conclusion that contest over the distribution of income, far from being neutral with respect to the environment, may have a significant effect on the quantity of residuals disposed of within the environment.

7.5   Economic conflict, environmental change, and uncertainty

An asymmetrical and time-varying power relationship between economic agents that is reflected in change in the distribution of the product may therefore be instrumental in generating externalities in all economies based on exactions or insertions into the environment. The effect of this will be to heighten the uncertainty discussed in Part III. We are once again led away from those approaches to human behavior that rest on the assumption of omnicompetence, suggesting that we need to rethink the theory of conflict and its implications for the time behavior of the system. More particularly, we need to locate conflict in the evolution of the system in a way that would have seemed natural to the classical political economists but now sounds very strange.

To those who believe that the theory of games gives a firm purchase on the nature of conflict this is a particularly unpalatable suggestion, but economic conflict is not a game with determinate rules and determinate outcomes (or at least determinate sets of possible outcomes). It is not conducted within the bounds of procedures known with absolute certainty. Indeed, as Shackle has pointed out time and again (1955, 1970, 1972), the theory of games assumes away the very thing that makes conflict worthwhile: the existence of speculative gains through the potential for surprise. Uncertainty in conflict is sufficient to ensure that there is no infallible algorithm for limiting the vulnerability of the parties to a contest. Apart from anything else, the infallibility of such an algorithm implies that the rules of the contest are not themselves affected by the actions of the contestants. But the rules of the game are not and cannot be known. The framework of human conflict cannot be perfectly seen ex ante. Indeed, the player who most successfully exploits that fact has the greatest advantage. In Shackle's terms, "the most dramatic and spectacular secret of success is novelty, and novelty is that which an infallible algorithm must, by definition, exclude" (1972, p. 426).

The framework of conflict in the global economy-environment system is the history of the system itself, and there is no reason at all to believe that it will ever be visible, ex ante. Economic conflict will necessarily change the rules of the contest by making unknown what was thought to be known, and by adding new twists and new conditions through the environmental effects of the disposals that follow the discarding of once-valued commodities. The rules of the contest are an evolving, partly signalled, partly anticipated set of boundary conditions that are highly sensitive to the nature of the contest. It follows that in a technologically dynamic economy subject to contest over the distribution of the product there is no reason to believe that the equilibrium state associated with any given technology or any given distribution of assets is actually attainable. Consequently, the existence of such equilibrium states is essentially uninteresting. What is interesting is the impact that the process of the convergence of the general system has on the signals of the economy, and the responses generated by those signals. In other words, what is interesting is not a mythical world-in-equilibrium, but the immediate impact on quantities and technology of the decisions made by agents in response to an evolving set of signals.

Patterns of investment, levels of economic activity, and technological change within the economy are not determined by an unattainable set of equilibrium signals, but by agents' intuitive feel for the likely evolution of the economic signals in the face of considerable uncertainty. Since those signals are, at best, very partial measures of the general system, they will necessarily give rise to unanticipated external effects, to novelty and surprise. These will then feed back into the system of signals, calling for new adjustments in the behavior of the system's agents. Change will beget change: the system will evolve in response to the process that Myrdal has called circular and cumulative causation. The notional equilibrium path associated with any one state of nature will very quickly be replaced by the notional equilibrium path associated with the next state. Indeed, the idea that the rules of historical contest can be known under such circumstances hardly seems worth discussion, and the notion that we can assume complete knowledge in conceptualizing human behavior in the global system seems nothing short of absurd.

PART III

Environmental strategies in an evolutionary economy-environment system

CHAPTER 8

Time, uncertainty, and external effects

8.1 Probability and surprise

The existence of environmental external effects supposes a time-dependent process of change that is not recorded in the price system. Because environmental external effects are always passed through an environmental process or processes, they always occur with a lag, arising after the decisions taken by agents on the basis of price signals. The distinction between the direct and indirect effects discussed by Meade is, as we have seen, a distinction between effects passed through a shorter or a longer environmental chain. It reflects what was called, in Chapter 3, the time distance between processes. Direct effects are more sharply focussed or less diffuse than indirect effects because of the length of the chain linking the processes at either end of an external effect.

Time is thus a necessary element in the generation of external effects. But what sort of time? As Georgescu-Roegen points out, there is a world of difference between "time" (with a small t) conceived as the mechanical measurement of an interval, and "Time" (with a capital T) conceived as "the stream of consciousness, or . . . a continuous succession of moments" (1971, p. 135). The length of the chain linking the processes at either end of an external effect certainly determines the interval between cause and effect, but is it the interval or the process it bounds that is important?

At various points in this essay we have made the assumption, for expositional purposes, that the system is time invariant or technologically stationary. Time is admitted under this assumption as if it were another dimension more or less equivalent to space. The system is assumed to be automatous, rolling on from period to period without visible change to its structure or inner workings. This is Georgescu-Roegen's time, the time of most economic dynamics. Yet the major inference to be drawn from the constructive model discussed in Chapter 2 is that the time invariance of the system contradicts the most fundamental physical laws of mass. The general system will not, indeed cannot, be time invariant. Any interval in the history of a far-from-equilibrium system must be associated with change in the physical characteristics of the system. Moreover, if we add the insight, again due to Georgescu-Roegen (1971, 1979), that change in the mass of resources organized within the limits of the entropy law is irreversible, then we preclude the possibility that the process of change is an ergodic one and so all future states of the system are statistically predictable. The time that is important to the understanding of external effects in an economy-environment system is Georgescu-Roegen's Time. It is what Carvalho has called "historical, irreversible, quality-changing 'Time'" (1983, p. 266).

What this means for the activities of agents, confronted by the necessity to make decisions based on an incomplete set of signals, is that the outcome of every action yielding an effect with some delay is shrouded in uncertainty. The problem of dealing with the environmental external effects of economic activity is, accordingly, a problem of coping with uncertainty, and the environmental strategies devised by different societies to do this reflect fundamental differences in assumptions made about the nature and significance of uncertainty.

To pave the way for our examination of such strategies it is useful to consider the points at issue in the treatment of uncertainty at the microeconomic level and to spell out the implications for uncertainty of the model identified here. These issues have recently been brought to the fore by the assurgence of interest in the rational expectations hypothesis constructed by Muth in the aftermath of Debreu's (1959) probabilistic approach to uncertainty in a general equilibrium system. They have, however, been the subject of a lifelong inquiry by Shackle (1949, 1955, 1961, 1972), as well as an enduring concern of Georgescu-Roegen (1971, 1976, 1979) and the Austrians (cf. Dolan, 1976).

The central point of dispute is the nature of knowledge about the future associated with the probabilistic approach to uncertainty. Both Shackle and Georgescu-Roegen have argued that wherever the range of possible outcomes of an action is known in advance, the problem is not one of uncertainty but of risk. Wherever the range of possible outcomes is not known in advance, there will be outcomes for which no pre-image exists. In other words, there exists what Georgescu-Roegen refers to as novelty and what Shackle calls surprise. Then and only then is it correct to speak of uncertainty.

The conceptualization of the bounds on the future associated with the probabilistic approach is therefore very different from that associated with uncertainty. The probabilistic approach assumes a remarkably complete knowledge of the future. "The role of probability arises when, [Shackle argues] because we cannot control Nature in the large or because we deliberately accept variability of circumstances in order to construct a game of chance, the circumstances can vary from one trial to another to a limited extent in a number of respects. It is then necessary to make a list between what we shall deem to be distinct outcomes, and this list must constitute an omni-competent classificatory system ... it follows that when the frequency-ratios which have been measured up to any stage of the process of observation are added together, they are bound to sum to unity" (1972, p. 18). The future states of a system are tantamount to rival hypotheses, only one of which can come true, and the procedure for attaching weights to each, "the procedure of subjective probabilities," supposes a perfect knowledge of its nature. It is a procedure which assumes that the list of rival hypotheses or subjective probabilities is complete. It assumes, with certainty, that no possible outcome has been left out of account. It is because the list of hypotheses is in fact endless and, as Shackle surmises, well beyond the imagination to construct, that the procedure of subjective probability is argued to be inappropriate.

To demonstrate this argument Shackle and others working within the same paradigm have sought to identify the necessary conditions for the future to be unknown. So Davidson, in criticizing the rational expectations hypothesis, notes that it supposes that information available to the decision-makers yields accurate knowledge of the probability distribution of actual outcomes today and for all future dates. (1982, p. 182). The future is assumed to be a stationary stochastic process; stochastic processes being stationary if the random variables are well defined for all points in time and if their cumulative probability distributions are independent of time. Thus "Nature is conceived of as throwing the die to select the events of the stochastic process which generates the realization being observed by each decision maker. Nature, it is therefore assumed, is making [what Lucas and Sargent had earlier called] 'independent drawings from a *fixed* probability distribution function'" (1982, p. 184). For the hypothesis to provide unbiased forecasts without persistent errors both the subjective and objective distributions must coincide, and the stochastic process must be ergodic – implying that the time and statistical (or space) averages of expectations must be the same. If the future is non-ergodic, the rational expectations hypothesis fails.

The existence of what Shackle calls crucial decisions by economic agents is therefore sufficient to ensure a non-ergodic world, since the essential characteristic of such decisions is that they involve irreversible, unforeseen, change. According to Shackle (1955), crucial or even contingently crucial experiments are, to all intents and purposes, unique and "never-to-be-repeated." Moreover, even when such experiments are not objectively incapable of repetition, they may be subjectively regarded as unique.

If there exist either objectively or subjectively crucial decisions, the result is a view of the future that allows little scope for a probabilistic interpretation. Crucial decisions generate surprise, and surprise implies uncertainty. The chief characteristics of uncertainty are thus that it involves the suspicion that the set of images we have of the future is incomplete: that those images do not offer an exhaustive list of possible outcomes of our actions. It involves doubt that the same images are in fact mutually exclusive. Even if new images are added, it implies no necessary change to the probability we might assign to the realization of all other images. In other words, uncertainty implies that our images of the future are not the complete set of rival hypotheses needed for the probabilistic approach. There is no reason to believe that we will not be surprised by the actual outcome of an activity, where experience is taken to cause surprise whenever there exists no pre-image of it. Indeed, it is more reasonable to suggest that we expect to be surprised by the outcome of our actions, implying that we attach zero potential surprise to the hypothesis that the outcomes of our actions will be different from those we have imagined.

Shackle's surprise is, in fact, very close to Georgescu-Roegen's novelty, though Georgescu-Roegen argues that novelty is a stronger concept than surprise in that while surprise involves some ex-ante belief in the possibility of surprise, novelty involves "ex-post surprise but not ex-ante belief in it" (1971, p. 123). Both authors are, however, led to a very similar concept of time and to a very similar conclusion as to the nature and significance of theories of real historical time. So Shackle makes a clear distinction between theories that are analytic and those that are constructive, the former describing situations or states of affairs, the latter describing steps or movements of transformation by which one situation is carried into others.

Analytic theories are argued to be equilibrium oriented and to deal only with knowable circumstances – which Shackle considers to be the immediate present. "Situations and events removed into the future are not observable, and thus not knowable, for there is no proof of any rigid implication of the future by the past, and such an implication would contradict the notion of originative choice" (1972, p. 53). Georgescu-Roegen's (1971) position on this is similar. Since the irreversibility of time is but another name for the irreversibility of entropic processes, and since the probabilistic interpretation of entropic processes has not been proved, the future is assumed not to be knowable from the past. Both authors accordingly argue the relevance of Shackle's constructive theories of the processes leading from notionally knowable present states to unknowable future states; theories informed by what Shackle calls the diachronic method, a method of uncovering the "broad current of self-determining, or organically evolving history."

The implication of this for our view of the decision-making process is immediate. There is no longer any reason to believe in the relevance or even the interest of deterministic models of optimization over time. "It is too much," Shackle writes, "to suppose that men can discover a set of biographies, one for each of them, such as would fit together in a pre-reconciled fashion and give to each of them the best he could get, subject to the equal freedom of other men to·seek their 'best.' The notion of a wholly foreseen and wholly constrained biography-to-come is nightmarish. . . . A general solution, or general equilibrium, has accordingly to be conceived as a state of affairs and not a course of affairs" (1972, p. 90). Although the rationality assumed in the optimizing approach is consistent with synchronic or static analysis, it has no meaning in the context of diachronic constructive theory. Time introduces change into technology, tastes, social organization, and policy, with the result that income distribution and market values simply lose all historical comparability in a short space of time.

This has not prevented attempts to model decision making under Knightian uncertainty. Arrow and Hurwicz (1972), for example, have insisted on the existence of optimality criteria for decision making under "complete ignorance" – defined as circumstances in which the consequence of an action is a function of an unknown state of nature drawn from an unknown set of such states. Like all choice algorithms, however, the Arrow-Hurwicz solution imposes sufficient knowledge to make decisions possible. Theirs is not complete ignorance at all. Indeed, where the future is not statistically uncoverable, and where the range of possible outcomes is unknown, the notion that it is possible to determine a set of actions that is intertemporally optimal both before and after the fact loses all meaning.

Yet agents do undertake activities according to a set of rules that discriminates between those that are, ex ante, efficient and those that are inefficient, between those that are expected to yield "desirable" outcomes, and those that are not. In other words, there are decision-making processes that admit, ex ante, the idea of optimization. Von Mises' peasant burning a candle to increase his crops is, in this sense, the same as the resource economist applying the Hotelling rule to optimize the rate of extraction of some mineral deposit. Neither ensure, ex post, the realization of optimal results, but both satisfy the requirement that we do our best. The difference between them lies only in the range of variables regarded as relevant and the linkages believed to exist between those variables.

8.2   Discounting time and uncertainty

The distinction between direct and indirect effects now acquires sharper significance. Recall that direct effects pass through a "shorter" environmental chain, and that indirect effects pass through a "longer" one. Direct effects are, by and large, subject to less uncertainty, implying that they are associated with less potential surprise, than indirect effects. Since the length of the environmental chain is a measure of the time delay in the transmission of external effects, it follows that the tractability of the problem of dealing with environmental external effects decreases with the length of the time horizon of the agents concerned. The discounting of time is at one and the same time the discounting of uncertainty.

This suggests that we need to reappraise the now conventional practice of separating the impacts of time and uncertainty. Burmeister (1980), for example, claims that it is "evident" that time plays two distinct roles. First, when future events are certain, the rationality of current behavior requires that agents take into account the existence of future states. This he calls the "pure role of time." Second, when future events are uncertain, time is important in accommodating that uncertainty. This he calls the role of uncertainty. Of course, under the rational expectations hypothesis the second role disappears since, as Burmeister points out, an equilibrium time path derived under the assumption of certainty is "identical to that arising in an uncertain world if the variables that were assumed to be known are replaced by their expected values (1980, p. 2). If we do not operate under a probabilistic approach, however, it is apparent that the two "roles" of time do no more than distinguish between direct and indirect effects. Put another way, the assumption of certainty that identifies the pure role of time is equivalent to the assumption that we are interested in what may be called the *environmental short period;* the period in which there is no environmental change associated with a particular action. The assumption of uncertainty is equivalent to the assumption that we are interested in the *environmental long period,* during which the process of environmental change has generated at least some external effects. The environmental short period may be thought of as the period in which it is legitimate to assume perfect foresight. The environmental long period is any period in which the assumption of perfect foresight does not hold.

The basic concept in the theory of decision making over time is the discount rate, or rate of time preference; the rate at which income earned in one period is preferred to income earned in the next. It is through the discount rate that it is possible to distinguish between the costs and revenues of a program of production, defined as a sequence of activities undertaken over a definite interval. By discounting future relative to present costs and revenues it is possible to weight the different phases of a program. More important, given that the uncertainty associated with a program increases with its duration, other things being equal, it follows that the discount rate similarly weights the uncertainty associated with that program. A low discount rate (which implies that income generated in the future generates a high weight relative to the present) admits a greater degree of uncertainty in a given program than a high discount rate (which implies a low weight on future income).

First, let us define a program for the ith activity in a time-varying system over the interval $[0,k]$ as

$$\left\{ \begin{array}{l} q_i(0)[\underline{\mathbf{b}}_i(0)E\mathbf{p}(1) - \underline{\mathbf{a}}_i(0)\mathbf{p}(0)], \\ E\{q_i(1)[\underline{\mathbf{b}}_i(1)\mathbf{p}(2) - \underline{\mathbf{a}}_i(1)\mathbf{p}(1)]\}, \\ \cdots\cdots\cdots\cdots\cdots\cdots\cdots\cdots\cdots\cdots\cdots\cdots \\ E\{q_i(k-1)[\underline{\mathbf{b}}_i(k-1)\mathbf{p}(k) - \underline{\mathbf{a}}_i(k-1)\mathbf{p}(k-1)]\} \end{array} \right\} \qquad 8.1$$

E denotes expected values. If we denote the private discount rate applied in the ith activity in the jth period by $d_i(j)$, then it follows that the expected net present value of the program is

$$\begin{aligned} EPV_i = {}& q_i(0)[\underline{\mathbf{b}}_i(0)E\mathbf{p}(1) - \underline{\mathbf{a}}_i(0)\mathbf{p}(0)]j \\ & + \sum_j E\{q_i(j)[\underline{\mathbf{b}}_i(j)\mathbf{p}(j+1) - \underline{\mathbf{a}}_i(j)\mathbf{p}(j)]\}[1 + d_i(j)]^{-j} \end{aligned}$$

$$j = 1, \ldots, k-1 \qquad 8.2$$

By attaching an appropriate decision rule (based on the assumption that no program will be undertaken for which the net present value is negative), this or an analogous measure of the present worth of a program extending into the future has historically been used to discriminate between projected programs in terms of given discount rates. The problem with the approach is that decisions taken on this basis are, as Scitovsky (1954) implicitly recognized, highly sensitive to the discount rate applied, and the choice of discount rate raises a number of very difficult questions. If the private and social rates of discount are different, decisions that are optimal in terms of a private analysis will not be optimal from the perspective of society, and vice versa. It is a problem made even more difficult by the fact that no simple rule exists for determining the optimal discount rate for society. Indeed, the selection of the discount rate in such analysis remains one of the thorniest problems in economics, since it raises entirely normative questions well beyond the reach of the discipline.

Whether we consider the private or social discount rate, it implies ethical judgments of a particularly significant kind. To emphasize this property of the social discount rate, Dasgupta and Heal characterize it as "a welfare term" pure and simple. It is a measure of the rate at which it is considered socially desirable to substitute consumption in some period for that in the next. It thus leads directly to the consideration of social judgments about intertemporal or intergenerational equity, and the appropriate form of intertemporal social welfare functions. An egalitarian or Rawlsian intertemporal social welfare function, for example, implies that the future may not be discounted at all. A utilitarian intertemporal social welfare function, on the other hand, implies that it may.

At issue is what responsibility the collectivity of the moment feels for the well-being of those who are to follow. A positive discount rate is not just an index of impatience (Koopmans, 1960) or an assertion of the sovereignty of present consumers (Marglin, 1963); it is evidence of a very general feeling that the future can look after itself to a greater or lesser degree. In other words, positive discount rate implies that a program may be adjudged optimal which, as Dasgupta and Heal put it, allows "the economy to decay in the long run" (1979, p. 299). It implies that the collectivity is not prepared to accept responsibility for the state of the system in future periods.

More particularly, the application of a positive discount rate in decision models based on 8.2 favors programs that yield high levels of income now, at the cost of low or even negative levels of income in the future. It thus implies that the impoverishment of future generations as a result of the profligacy of present generations is not just an incidental, but a desirable outcome. By contrast, where the future is not discounted, as is the case under an egalitarian intertemporal social welfare function, programs are only optimal if they yield a constant income stream in all periods. The criterion of such a welfare function, the maximization of the minimum period-income, requires a program that delivers maximum constant income.

The salient points here are that the choice of a social discount rate involves matters of ethics and judgment, and that different ethics will result in the choice of different sets of programs of production. Add to this that the choice of discount rate also involves the allowance to be made for environmental effects that are uncertain in their incidence and it becomes clear just how far removed the social discount rate is from an objective measure of the value of capital. But nor is the private discount rate applied by individual economic agents any less divorced from judgments about responsibility for the future. Private discounting of the income stream of the future also means discounting the future effects of present activities, or discounting the possibility of novelty or surprise where those effects are uncertain. It implies indifference to the possibility that present actions will make the future a minefield of latent external effects.

8.3   Structure, time preference, and external effects

The existence of external effects is, as we have seen, a function of the incompleteness of markets, and thus the fact that market prices are inadequate observers of the general system. The point has been made, though, that external effects need not be unanticipated or unseen, except in the narrow sense that they are unobserved through the price system. To see the importance of the discount rate for the generation of external effects under the intertemporal optimization of programs of production, consider those effects that, because the structure of the system is such that the environmental chain is clear, are physically observable. Noise nuisance from a single source would be an example on the side of pollution. Although it is readily detectable by the physical senses, it is almost invariably beyond the reach of the price system. Land degradation through overcropping or overgrazing would be an example on the side of depletion. The processes at either end of the environmental chain are unambiguously identified, and the chain is well defined.

To isolate the role of time preference from the political relations implicit in the definition of external effects, we may ignore the costs or benefits of such an action to other producers and consider the own-effects only. The question is thus whether to undertake an action expected to have own-effects in the future. It it is optimal to risk severely adverse own-effects in the future, it may be assumed to be optimal to risk effects on others. It may be seen that even where such effects are directly observable they may be ignored simply because they are fully discounted wherever the exigencies of the present override those of the future. The decision to undertake a program may be optimal, but still lead to disaster for those concerned.

It should be noted that this is independent of the nature of property rights. There may be either private property in the means of production or some form of collective property – either common or communal. If there is private property, then we are considering the individual agent's own decision-making process. If there is communal or common property, then the decision-making process of the collectivity is involved. More particularly, we are considering the determinants of the private or social value placed on current over future consumption: the private or social rate of time preference.

From 5.1 and 5.2 the *net income* accruing to the agents of the economy in the first period may be defined as

$$y(0) = Dq(0)[B(0)p(1) - A(0)p(0)] \qquad\qquad 8.3$$

and in subsequent periods

$$y(k) = Dq(k)[B(k)p(k + 1) - A(k)p(k)] \qquad k = 1,2, \ldots \qquad 8.4$$

The present value of the ith program, assuming that it yields a net income stream known with certainty over k periods from a given technology and assuming a constant discount rate, may be defined by

$$PV_i(0,k) = y_i(0) + \sum_j y_i(j)[1 + d_i]^{-j} \qquad j = 1, \ldots, k - 1 \qquad 8.5$$

Suppose that the activity of the ith producer(s) in any one period has feedback effects external to the price system that are subject to a delay determined by the structure of the system. Every activity thus has direct current costs, known with certainty, and expected indirect costs in terms of income foregone in the future as a result of negative external effects. These indirect costs represent expected changes in the technology of the process resulting from the effects of current economic activities on the environment. We can show the expected present value of the net income stream over k periods as

$$EPV_i(0,k) = E\{y_i(0) + \sum_j y_i(j)[1 + d_i]^{-j}\} \qquad j = 1, \ldots, k - 1 \qquad 8.6$$

where E, as before, denotes expected values.

Since the lagged expected indirect costs of current activity will be discounted in exactly the same way as other future benefits and costs, the longer the lags and the higher the rate of time preference, the lower the weight given to potential future damage associated with current output. If the rate of time preference is high enough, it will be quite conceivable that current activities in the ith process expected to have the effect of incurring net losses in the next few periods will still be undertaken. Indeed, when we endogenize the rate of time preference, it is easy to see the circumstances in which this will be rational behavior.

To take an extreme example, consider the behavior of agents operating at or near the minimum subsistence level, as many agricultural producers in the underdeveloped countries are. If we define the minimum subsistence income of the ith producer(s) to be y_i^*, then we can determine the minimum rate of time preference compatible with the satisfaction of that level of income, d_i^*. More particularly, if we write

$$EPV_i(0,k) = \min\{y_i(0), y_i^*\} + \sum_j Ey_i(j)[1 + d_i]^{-j} \qquad j = 1, \ldots, k = 1$$

$$8.7$$

then recalling the definition of $y(k)$ from 8.4, if we define $q_i^*(0)$ to be the minimum level of activity necessary to yield y_i^* for the given price vector $p(0)$ and the expected price vector $p(1)$, then d_i^* will be the solution to

$$q_i^*(0)[\underline{b}_i(0)p(1) - \underline{a}_i(0)Ep(0)] = - \sum_j E\{q_i(k)[\underline{b}_i(j)p(j + 1)$$

$$- \underline{a}_i(k)p(j)]\}[1 + d_i^*]^{-j} \qquad j = 1, \ldots, k - 1 \qquad 8.8$$

From our assumption $y_i(j)$ becomes negative and of increasing absolute value as j approaches k. 8.8 accordingly implies that the minimum rate of time preference will be such that the future costs of the current level of activity in excess of the minimum subsistence income are completely discounted. The minimum rate of time preference may therefore be thought of as a poverty-determined discount rate. Where, for example, agricultural producers are constrained as to their choice of technique, and where the set of input and output prices facing them has the effect of driving the minimum activity level upwards, it is very easy to see how the choice between starving today or starving tomorrow can lead to a ruinously high rate of time preference. The nature of property rights in these circumstances is irrelevant. Nor do I suppose that individual agents are unaware of the likely impact of their activities. They are, however, compelled to discount both expected future costs and benefits to the point where all that matters is survival in the next period. The immediate source of the problem in this example is the inelasticity of short-run demand, and any circumstance that exaggerates this will act to raise the discount rate applied to programs involving long-period environmental costs. Whether the environmental costs of a particular program are immediate or deferred is, however, a function of the structure of the system – the time distance or length of the environmental chain between an action and its effect.

8.4   Investment, waste, and external effects

We are very clearly at the edge of the modern theory of external effects here, but it is worth recalling that this is in fact where it began. Scitovsky's (1954) paper on the so-called pecuniary external effects focussed on the long-period effects of investment in economic systems. He argued that investment of any sort indicated the existence of positive rates of profit and that this showed the system to be away from equilibrium. More important, investment had the effect of driving the system further away from equilibrium in the future. Since investment was undertaken on the basis of current market prices, and since these were unable to signal the conditions obtaining in the future, investment would necessarily be associated with unanticipated and unobserved effects.

Scitovsky's concerns are neatly summarized in the following passage:

In the market economy, prices are the signalling device that informs each person of other people's economic decisions; and the merit of perfect competition is that it would cause prices to transmit information reliably and people to respond to this information properly. Market prices, however, reflect the economic situation as it is and not as it will be. For this reason, they are more useful for coordinating current production decisions, which are immediately effective and guided by short-run considerations than they are for coordinating investment decisions, which have a delayed effect and – looking ahead to a long future period – should be governed not by what the present economic situation is but by what the future economic situation is expected to be. The proper coordination of investment decisions, therefore, would require a signalling device to transmit information about present plans and future conditions as they are determined by present plans; and the pricing system fails to provide this (1954, p. 150).

It is interesting that even in 1954 the ground was being prepared for expectations to provide a "solution" to this problem. In a footnote to the passage, Scitovsky acknowledges a suggestion by Arrow that futures markets would be sufficient to provide such a set of signals, but while it is true that in a competitive economy a complete set of futures markets would accurately signal expectations about the future, the thrust of Scitovsky's argument was that the average private planning horizon was too short to pick up the socially important long-period effects of investment.

There are, in fact, two distinct issues being broached in the passage. One is the non-existence of adequate signals to inform investment programs extending into the future, and the other is the timing of the effects of any given investment. The first issue bears on many of the questions raised in this essay – about the nature of the value system, the separate influences of market and political power, the linkages between economy and environment, and the existence and the nature of uncertainty. The second issue, however, bears directly on the discount rate. The focus of Scitovsky's argument was that the anticipation of the long-period effects of investment required central planning and coordination. The collectivity alone was, in the absence of an appropriate signalling system, capable of anticipating the relevant effects. Scitovsky was not explicit about this, but it is hard to resist the inference that part of the reason was that the collectivity not only could but should take a longer view than the individuals within it. If this is so, it would make Scitovsky's concerns similar to those of Ramsey (1928) who considered social discounting to be ethically indefensible.

What is important for our purposes is that investments were recognized to have cumulative effects in the long period that were claimed to drive the system away from equilibrium. This makes the decision to invest crucial in Shackle's sense. It is a decision that involves irreversible change. What we can add to Scitovsky's view, therefore, is that the long-period effects of investment will not be known at the moment the decision to invest is made, no matter what signals are employed. The long-period effects of investment will entail surprise. Whether the possibility of these effects is recognized or ignored depends on the discount rate applied, and a similar ethic would demand that the collectivity not only could but should do everything possible to anticipate these effects.

Scitovsky's insistence on the importance of time in the theory of external effects was not subsequently taken up in the literature, and attention reverted to a quintessentially static approach in which time featured only as Georgescu-Roegen's mechanical, locomotive time. Moreover, while the question of the discount rate became of pervading, even obsessive interest in the theory of exhaustible resource depletion, it was all but ignored in the microeconomics of economy-environment interactions.

This compartmentalization of ideas has, however, been particularly unhelpful. The relation between an economy and its environment is an integrated dynamic process in which Georgescu-Roegen's Time and uncertainty are the central features. The programs of production undertaken by individual economic agents are merely strands in this process, each associated with a set of intertemporal effects that is unknown and unknowable at the outset precisely because of the indecomposability of the system. It is to make sense of the unknowable that agents adopt decision-making procedures prescribing the range of "relevant" variables, with the criterion of relevance used to exclude aspects of the process that are awkward to deal with, and to include those that are tractable. There is, in fact, no stronger arbiter of relevance than the preferred limits of our forward vision, our planning horizon and rate of time preference. It is more powerful even than the notion of spatial or territorial limits of responsibility that discriminates between relevant and irrelevant effects on the basis of geographically defined property rights. As was argued in Section 3.5, the myopic decomposition of the system is the only credible rationale for treating economic processes as if they were independent of their environment. However, the fact that an individual agent may declare the future to have a zero weight does not mean that the future effects of present actions will not occur. All it means is that they will be unanticipated and unobserved. External effects are an increasing function of the rate of time preference.

Finally, it is worth remarking that the same compartmentalization of ideas has been unhelpful in another way. Investment is, in fact, merely one form of the disposal of residuals which it was argued in Chapter 2 account for the evolutionary nature of far-from-equilibrium economy-environment systems. Economically, investment describes the allocation of residuals to the processes of the economy in order to augment the expected value of the outputs of those processes. Physically, it can be thought of as the commitment of economic resources to secure possession of some environmental resource. But there are other types of residual that, formally, are no different from investment. There are, for instance, the waste products of the processes of the economy. Both waste and investment represent material resources surplus to current requirements, and their allocation among the processes of the system will be associated with change. Although the observability of the processes of the economy may be superior to that of its environment, both investment and waste disposal will involve unobserved effects over time. In both cases the agents making the allocations will be acting speculatively, guessing at the gains and losses to be made from holding or disposing of assets against an uncertain future. That, at least, has been the economic experience so far. Over three hundred years ago, Cantillon described the activity of the business executive as involving the purchase of assets at a known price with a view to selling them at a price that, at the moment of their purchase, is unknown. Nothing has changed. Economics is still about speculative activity in the face of uncertainty, and whether we are considering acts of investment (depletion) or waste disposal (pollution), the notion of perfect foresight or omnicompetence has no place whatsoever.

CHAPTER 9

The market solution

9.1 Resource depletion and pollution

We come now to the point where we can assess what has been called the market solution to the twin environmental problems generated by the process of economic growth: the depletion of environmental resources and the pollution of environmental processes. This returns us to the questions raised in Chapter 4 in connection with the Club of Rome debate of the early 1970s. How are we to assess the theory of optimal depletion and pollution in an evolutionary economy-environment system subject to uncertainty? What are we to make of the reliance on general equilibrium models to yield efficient solutions to the problems of the despoliation of a far-from-equilibrium real world? To begin, let us rehearse the purely physical reasons for the significance of depletion and pollution in an economy-environment system.

It has already been remarked that the depletion of environmental resources is synonymous with exactions on the environment, where an exaction is defined as the forcible, uncompensated, acquisition of the outputs of one process by the agent(s) of another process. Whether the rate of exactions on environmental resources at any particular moment in the history of the system is greater than or less than the rate of regeneration of those same resources determines whether the depletion problem is popularly considered to be an exhaustible or renewable resource problem. Strictly, we have defined environmental resources subject to exaction to be renewable under a given technology if their maximum potential own-rate of growth is greater than or equal to the maximum potential own-rate of growth of the economy, and to be exhaustible if their maximum potential own-rate of growth is less than that of the economy. Depletion, in this sense, is significant because resources have two properties.

The first of these properties is that *matter is heterogeneous*. It is intuitive that the heterogeneity of resources explains why we should be interested in the problem of scarcity or in the behavior of prices that distinguish one resource from another. The specific properties of the resources available to the system at a given moment in its history, and the way that those properties match the requirements of the production and consumption technologies then applied, determine their utility or use value. If all resources were perfect substitutes, implying that all resources had the same properties, there would be no point in discriminating between them. What is significant for the idea of depletion is that the heterogeneity of resources is also sufficient cause to believe that the complementarity of resources is a better first approximation of the relation between resources than substitutability. So long as we suspend belief in our own evolution, we have to suppose that each resource is not a substitute for all others, even in the long period. We cannot, to give a crude example, envisage the substitution of lead, uranium, or mercury for wheat, rice, or cassava as a staple in the human diet. The heterogeneity of resources under less than perfectly flexible production and consumption technology means that the exhaustion of resources is not only possible, but may be economically significant.

The second property is that *matter degrades*. As Georgescu-Roegen has argued, and as has been pointed out above, matter, like energy, degrades from useful to unuseful forms. All material transformations are characterized by the fact that material inputs are used up in the process. This does not, of course, mean that the mass of resources advanced in the process diminishes. But by exploiting the properties of a resource of given mass that make it useful under some recipe, the future utility of that mass under the same recipe is diminished. It may still have utility under some other recipe, but just as there are no perdurable means of production, there are no means of production that yield a constant flow of utility under a given technology. In the absence of perfect recycling, it follows that production under any recipe implies continuous drawings on the raw materials required by that recipe.

On the other side of the environmental problem, pollution has been identified with insertions into the environment; recalling that an insertion is defined as the forcible, uncompensated, imposition by the agent(s) of one process of the outputs of that process on another process. We have seen that the wastes of one set of processes are the pollutants of another. More particularly, in an economy-environment system the wastes – both economic and noneconomic – of the economy are the pollutants of the environment. It should be recalled that economic wastes are unemployed economic (and so positively valued) resources, and that noneconomic wastes are the zero-valued outputs of economic processes.

The property of waste that makes pollution of potential significance is that wastes are seldom, if ever, completely inert. Both types of waste are defined by the fact that they have no positive role to play in the processes of the economy. The properties that made the original raw materials useful under the technology applied have been used up, or are surplus to requirements. But this does not mean that they may have no role in other processes. Indeed, the waste products of economic processes typically have properties that make them of considerable significance in the processes of the environment.

To put this another way, notice that the heterogeneity of matter referred to relates to the distinctive chemical and physical properties of a resource that enable it, when combined with other resources in some definite recipe, to do "work" of some definite form. That potential to do work is an essential element in determining the utility of a resource. In the productive processes of the economy, the energy potential of the different material resources used in a recipe determines the intensity if not the form of the services that each can yield. The existence of some energy potential is thus a necessary condition for a resource to have positive utility and so positive value, and diminution of that potential implies the diminution of the usefulness of the resource.

To see the environmental implications of this, note that economic processes, just as all other processes, are entropy producing. That is, they will be associated with a decrease in the ability of the resources employed to do useful work. Any process of production, considered as a thermodynamic process, generates heat that is wasted in the sense that it cannot be recovered to do further work without the expenditure of an even greater amount of energy. The waste heat of an economic process is the thermal energy potential of the products of that process that have no economic value or, put another way, have diminished ability to perform (economically) useful work. What is environmentally significant about this is that if the insertion of such products into the processes of the environment creates a thermal gradient, it will have a qualitative effect on the outputs of those processes, just as it will if the same waste products are of a chemical composition or physical structure that causes them to react to the environmental resources with which they are combined. These effects may range from the complete transformation of inorganic environmental resources to more subtle metabolic or neurophysical alterations in the organisms of the environment.

The point of recalling these features of depletion and pollution is to underscore the fact that both concepts describe material flows across the boundaries between the economy and its environment. Both depletion and pollution involve direct intervention by economic agents in the processes of the environment, and this intervention is not mediated by the signals of the economy. What we consider in this chapter, the optimal depletion and pollution policies of the market solution, has nothing at all to say about the specifics of such intervention because it has nothing to say about possession and control. Our concern here is with the use of economic as opposed to physical signals to accommodate the affects of such direct intervention in the environment, and the importance of judgments about the significance of present relative to future activity in modifying the economic signals.

9.2   The market solution: elements of an environmental strategy

The dominant environmental strategy of the market economies of the West, what I have called the market solution, is primarily the product of the libertarian approach to economics that has its roots in Chicago, though with some lingering remnants of Pigouvian welfare theory. Two related judgments underpin this strategy, both already alluded to. The first is the judgment that it is proper to discount the future effects of present activities at a positive rate. The second is that it is proper to seek the appropriate discount rate in the current transactions between private economic agents.

The widespread acceptance of both judgments by the economics profession is of comparatively recent origin. Until the 1960s the thrust of the mainstream of economic literature was antipathetic to the notion of discounting. Ramsey (1928), Pigou (1932), and Harrod (1948) are perhaps the best known critics of discounting, Ramsey having scathingly referred to "a practice which is ethically indefensible and arises merely from the weakness of the imagination" (1928, p. 543). Fisher suggests that their position was anticipated by most of the Cambridge moral philosophers and economists between 1885 and 1925 (1981, pp. 68–69), though Sidgwick's concession to the propriety of discounting for uncertainty dates from 1890. By the mid 1960s, however, the disapprobation of discounting among economists had all but disappeared. The way was cleared for the evolution of the market solution.

There is clearly no single cause of this about face, but it does seem to be associated with a change in our perceptions of two phenomena: technology and the state. Take technology first. There has certainly been a marked shift in economists' attitudes toward technology and the potential substitutability of resources. If we consider, for example, a very early and remarkable study of exhaustible resources, Jevons' examination of the depletion of British coal reserves in 1865, we are struck by his technological pessimism. Jevons firmly predicted the complete exhaustion of British coal reserves while avowing the "impossibility of finding a substitute" (1906, p. x). That is very different from the optimism that marks even the most cautious of modern studies in the mainstream of resource economics. One explanation for the change in attitude might be the unprecedented surge in innovative activity in the management and production of fossil fuels in the first half of this century, a development that made a mockery of Jevons' predictions. But the evidence in fact suggests that the emergence of a strong technological optimism among economists is of more recent vintage, paralleling the work on dynamic models in the 1960s. The most powerful statements in support of the capacity of future generations to cope with problems bequeathed by past generations have come only in the wake of the Club of Rome debate. Of these the boldest by far is that of Marchetti (1980) who, having noticed that a series of major technological advances since the mid-nineteenth century had seen the substitution of a succession of fossil fuels, each with a higher net energy yield than the last, infers that with such ingenuity at our disposal we need have no fears of being bound by environmental constraints resulting from the exhaustion of raw materials. The limits to growth may be adroitly sidestepped just as they begin to loom menacingly, and Marchetti, though less reserved than most, is by no means alone in holding this view.

What is interesting about the new technological optimism is its links with the theory of growth and depletion. Beckerman's laconic comment, "I am sure that we will think up something" summarizes a view that is much more than a casual belief in human ingenuity. It is the necessary adjunct to the assumption that in the long period substitutes exist for all exhaustible resources: that his "incentives to new exploration, recycling, and the use of substitutes, that would all be occurring gradually as the increasing scarcity of any product led to an upward trend in its price," already referred to, would bear fruit in the real world. The substitutability of resources, it should be remembered, is an axiom of the static Walrasian system – reflected in assumptions about the nature of the production function. It comes as something of a surprise to find that something as woolly as the belief that "we will think of something" turns out to have similarly axiomatic status in the intertemporal models of modern resource economists.

In 1974 Solow established that the survival of an economy using an exhaustible resource, but in which there existed an augmentable or inexhaustible substitute, depended on the elasticity of substitution between the two. He showed that consumption could be maintained indefinitely under the assumptions of costless extraction and constant elasticities of substitution if either the elasticity of substitution was greater than one or, if equal to one, that the elasticity of output of the inexhaustible resource was greater than that of the exhaustible resource. It hardly needs repeating that no resource can be regarded as indefinitely augmentable. In the long run the conservation of mass condition rules all. But given the heterogeneity of matter it was obviously an interesting question to ask how far substitutability between resources could relieve the constraint imposed by the scarcity of a given resource. It is a short step from Solow's result to the construction of a model that assumes the technological change necessary to ensure the substitutability of all resources. Such a model is to be found in Kemp et al. (1984), where it is shown that providing that innovation increases with the level of investment, Solow's result is really quite general. The transition from general technological optimism to the axiom of the intertemporal substitutability of resources under as-yet-to-be-discovered technologies is complete.

The second change in perception referred to is the change in our perception of the role of the state that has followed the collapse of the Keynesian system and the emergence of the new economic liberalism. This has involved a number of things, the most important of which, for purposes of this essay, seems to be the attitude to the social discount rate. Among the lesser effects, however, has been a reinterpretation of the significance of Pareto optimality as a criterion for judging the desirability of various economic outcomes. The inherently atomistic bias of the Pareto criterion appears to have become increasingly apparent, with the Pareto criterion being argued to support a much more decentralized decision-making procedure. Individual not social preferences matter. This is slightly ironical given the history of welfare theory. The Pigouvian tradition of state intervention to correct environmental external effects through a system of taxes and subsidies did, after all, appeal to the Pareto criterion. However, the inconsistency in this is exactly what has enabled the proponents of the Coaseian approach to make such gains in the last decade.

It has been argued that as the margin between social and private costs of depletion or pollution widens, so too will the propensity for markets in the relevant external effects to develop entirely independently. Dahlman, for example, criticizes Pigou for the assumption that where a negative environmental external effect exists the private costs of exacting compensation from the perpetrator exceeds the benefits, arguing that Pigou fails to demonstrate that "there is good reason for assuming that somebody else, outside the market, can do it better"

(1979, p. 154). The implication is that if neither the state nor any other nonmarket agency can do it better, then there is no difference between private and social cost and so no cause for believing an external effect to exist. The whole Pigouvian tradition is alleged to rest on an ideological assumption that the state has privileged knowledge of the Pareto optimal outcome, and is better equipped, informationally, to achieve it.

What is not noticed by Dahlman, though, is that the raison-d'être of state intervention in a Pigouvian world goes far beyond the Pareto criterion. It is the assumption that the state is, as Marglin put it in his celebrated denunciation of Pigou, "the guardian of the interests of future generations as well as the interests of the present generation" (1963, p. 97). For this reason the state adopts a lower discount rate than would be obtained from "a competitive market distillation of individual time-preference maps," given that individuals of necessity have a socially irrational attitude to their own deaths. The difference between the social and private rates of time preference authorizes the Pigouvian state to assume privileged knowledge.

The rejection of this view of the state reflects the assurgent economic liberalism that is, as already indicated, one of the key elements in the market solution. The notion that the appropriate discount rate can be obtained from current market transactions is tantamount to an assertion that individuals know not only what is best for them, but what is best for society as well. Playing what he described as "the bourgeois-democratic game of philosophical liberalism," Marglin declared it to be "axiomatic that a democratic government reflects only the preferences of the individuals who are presently members of the body politic" with the inference that so long as present members are indifferent to the claims of future individuals "a democratic view of the state does not countenance government intervention on behalf of future generations" (1963, pp. 97–8).

The Coase view is merely an extreme statement of the same position, holding that external effects generated as a result of imperfect information are better handled by direct contest between the parties involved than by the imposition of state penalties on the party who is the obvious source of the external effect. Dahlman again: "the real significance of the court cases cited by Coase is that the distinction between emittor and recipient of an external effect is irrelevant: what matters is whether we achieve a higher valued output by putting the liability on one or the other of the parties involved, and not who is the 'source' of the external effect. Since at least two parties are necessarily involved, either may be considered the source" (1979, p. 159). The victim, as various critics of Coase have observed, is always an accessory to the crime.

This combination of economic liberalism and technological optimism has resulted in an environmental strategy founded on a private perspective on time, the abnegation of collective responsibility for the future, and the denial of the significance of resource availability constraints in any meaningful time frame. Of course, the three notions are mutually supportive, since the meaningful time frame necessarily contracts as the discount rate goes up. This strategy, the market solution, has seen the traditional Pigouvian taxes and subsidies reduced to supplementary measures invoked only where it proves impossible for one reason or another to create a market for external effects. The dominant decision-making processes are microeconomic processes in which the relevant discount rate is the private rate. If the state intervenes, it is only to ameliorate the worst excesses of private individuals, and only where these excesses cannot be dealt with by market transaction. The central argument of the Pigouvian approach – that the collectivity has a responsibility to ensure the sustainability of the system of production, distribution, and exchange – has been more or less abandoned. Otherwise eclectic authors like Fisher (1981) are increasingly inclined to weigh the merits of private versus public handling of environmental issues on the scales of which can do better under an implicitly shared discount rate.

9.3   Optimal depletion

To tease out the implications of the arguments of this essay for the market solution, it is useful to consider in more detail the microeconomic decision-making processes designed to uncover the best depletion and pollution rates. Since we are interested in the properties of the basic models only, we may ignore the myriad variants of the models to be found in the literature (for which see, for example, Dasgupta and Heal, 1979, Fisher, 1981, and Kemp and Long, 1984).

The core of the theory of optimal environmental management lies in the theory of optimal depletion. The natural affinity of depletion and pollution theory has not, by and large, been recognized in the literature. As we will see, however, the basic depletion model has a readily recognizable counterpart in the theory of pollution. In its modern form, optimal depletion theory can be traced to a paper by Hotelling (1931), whose incorporation of the notion of discounting at a time when it was generally frowned upon may be the reason that the paper was almost completely ignored for thirty years. The key concept in the Hotelling theory of optimal depletion is that depletion is an activity in which the opportunity cost of production today is production at some future date. The Hotelling rule states that for an agent to be indifferent between extracting a resource (with zero extraction costs) in one period or the next, the sale price of that resource in the second period should be greater than its price in the first period by a factor equal to the expected rate of return obtainable from holding any other asset. Formally, if the alternative asset – the numeraire – is indexed j, the Hotelling rule requires that under costless extraction the time path of the price of the ith exhaustible resource will be given by

$$p_i(k + 1) = p_i(k)(1 + w_j) \qquad\qquad 9.1$$

since $p_i(k)$ units of the numeraire held from the kth to the $k + 1$th period are worth $p_i(k)(1 + w_j)$ units in the $k + 1$th period. To repeat, the Hotelling rule stipulates that the condition for an agent to be indifferent between holding or extracting a costlessly produced resource is that the capital gain earned on the resource must be equal to the return on any other asset. If we define the numeraire to be an interest-bearing asset, then the undiscounted *royalty price* of the depleted resource must rise at the rate of interest.

The royalty price requires a word of explanation. It has been argued previously that the necessary condition for a resource to be positively valued is that it be "possessed," by which is meant that positively valued inputs are advanced in its production. The royalty price is an apparent exception, since it attaches to resources that are exacted from the environment. It is the unextracted price of the resource. The exception is, however, more apparent than real. The royalty price in fact represents a claim on the sale price of the produced resource, in the same way as rentals accruing to the proprietors of other produced resources. The only difference is that the royalty price reflects the natural scarcity of a resource in finite supply. In this sense it defines the *user cost* of the resource, or the future opportunity cost of its extraction today.

In terms of the model developed in this work, a result that is equivalent to the Hotelling rule can be seen to follow from the optimization of a program of production. Consider such a program in the ith process extending over the interval $[0,k]$. We will assume that the technology of the ith process is constant in this interval, although the technology of the system as a whole may be time varying. The general system is assumed to decompose as in 6.10 and 6.11. The optimization problem is the following:

$$\max \Sigma_i q_i(t)[\underline{b}_i p(t + 1) - \underline{a}_i p(t)][1 + d_i]^{-t} \quad t = 0, \ldots, k - 1 \qquad 9.2$$

where d_i is the rate of discount applied in the ith process, assumed to be constant over the interval $[0,k]$. The vectors $\mathbf{p}$ are positive in their first h components only. Let the nth resource be a nonproduced environmental resource in finite supply, implying that $a_{nn}(t) = 0$ and $b_{nn}(t) = 1$ for all $t \in \{1, \ldots, k - 1\}$. 9.2 is then subject to

$$\Sigma_s q_i(s)a_{in} \leq q_n(t) \quad s = 0, \ldots, t; t = 0, \ldots, k - 1 \qquad 9.3$$

From the Lagrangean form of the function

$$L = \Sigma_i q_i(t)[\underline{b}_i p(t + 1) - \underline{a}_i p(t)][1 + d_i]^{-t} + \Sigma_t \gamma(t)[q_n(t) - \Sigma_s q_i(s)a_{in}]$$
$$s = 0, \ldots, t; t = 0, \ldots, k - 1 \qquad 9.4$$

we can see, by differentiating with respect to $q_i(t)$, that the necessary condition for a maximum where the environmental constraints are binding is that

$$\underline{b}_i p(t + 1) = \gamma(t)a_{in}[1 + d_i]^{-t} + \underline{a}_i p(t) \qquad 9.5$$

The optimal depletion rate will be such that in each period the unit value of output of the ith process will be equal to the sum of the costs of production and the undiscounted royalty price or the user cost of the nth environmental resource, $\gamma(t)a_{in}[1 + d_i]^{-t}$. Put another way, the arbitrage condition ensures that the profit-maximizing agent will adopt a depletion rate which ensures that the unit income generated in each period is exactly equal to the undiscounted royalty price of the depletable resource on which the process depends. The distribution of the royalty, of course, is a separate issue.

If extraction costs are constant, this yields a time path for the price of the resource with the usual characteristics: namely, that the royalty price of the scarce resource becomes an increasing proportion of the price of the extracted product. This is usually interpreted to mean that as time passes and the depleted resource gets increasingly scarce, so the scarcity rent element in the output price rises. It is, however, worth noting that this is a result that holds only in long-period equilibrium. In a far-from-equilibrium world relative price movements due to technological change or a distributional contest within the other $h - 1$ processes of the economy may generate offsetting increases in the input prices of the ith process. If this is so, there is no reason to believe that, other things being equal, extraction costs will rise more slowly than the royalty price.

Of the numerous other caveats on the basic Hotelling result explored in the literature, one in particular seems to be worth pursuing in the light of the arguments of this essay. As with all microeconomic decision-making models, the optimal depletion models address only the questions that seem to be of economic significance to the decision maker at the moment the decision is made. But precisely because of their dependence on exactions from the environment, extractive industries are especially prone to uncertainty. The royalty price on any one resource does not, after all, reflect an accurate knowledge of unextracted global resources. How the decision maker copes with uncertainty in the extractive industries is thus of particular interest. There are two standard techniques for doing this. The first is through the selection of appropriate discount rates, the second is through the accommodation of risk in contingent markets.

Leaving aside the question of the discount rate for the moment, the accommodation of risk through contingent markets is equivalent to the recognition only of probabilistic "uncertainty." It is, for example, stated that a complete set of Arrow-Debreu contingent markets covering commodities delivered at all future dates and in all states of nature would be sufficient to eliminate the problem. So they would. But while it is recognized that such a set of contingent markets does not exist, it is rarely observed that they cannot exist (except in the sense that future unborn generations are necessarily unrepresented in the market). The real problem is not one of risk – which may be satisfied by trading on contingent markets – but of uncertainty in the sense of Knight, Shackle, and Georgescu-Roegen: uncertainty that denies the possibility of the precognition of future states of nature and asserts the necessity of novelty and surprise. The reason for this is simple. In an interdependent economy-environment system future commodity production depends not only on present economic activities, but on the whole range of unobserved environmental effects that are external to the price system. The very concept of a complete set of Arrow-Debreu contingent markets, however, assumes away the possibility of unanticipated effects stemming from the generation of waste or the disruption of environmental processes through the extraction of natural resources.

It follows that the only means left of accommodating uncertainty is the discount rate. It has already been argued here that the discounting of time means the discounting of uncertainty, since uncertainty is an increasing function of time. In the special case where uncertainty does not increase over time, Fisher (1981) following Lewis (1976) has pointed out that the discount rate will be unaffected by uncertainty. It is, however, in the nature of an evolutionary system that the potential for surprise in a program of production increases with the time horizon of the program, while the utility of contingent markets decreases. What is more important is that there is reason to believe in a positive feedback between uncertainty and the discount rate. Recall that uncertainty is a function of systemic changes as a result of residuals disposals in both the economy and the environment, and that residuals increase with the level of activity. It follows then that a high discount rate that raises the current rate of exploitation of environmental resources will be associated with increasing levels of disposals, increasing environmental change, increasing uncertainty, and consequent higher discount rates in the future. High discount rates thus feed the counterpart to the problem of depletion, the problem of pollution.

9.4   Optimal pollution

The modern theory of optimal pollution control is of more recent vintage than the theory of optimal depletion, but it continues to reflect a Pigouvian influence that is almost nonexistent in the theory of depletion. The major early contributions to the modern literature, by Boulding (1966), Ayres and Kneese (1969), and Kneese, Ayres, and d'Arge (1970), argued that the increase in the wastes generated in expanding the production of economic goods had created an all-embracing problem of pollution that the price system was ill equipped to handle. Unlike the predictions of the Doomsday Models, these arguments found ready acceptance among economists. Indeed, comments such as the following remark by Baumol and Oates are now commonplace: "external effects [resulting from waste disposals] pervade virtually every sector of our economy; they are an unavoidable element of the production process; and their consequences tend to grow disproportionately with increasing population and the expansion of the economy's activities" (1979, p. 77).

The problem addressed in the optimal pollution control models is to determine the optimal amount of pollutants that may be released in the course of an economic activity by some criterion. As critics of the approach have pointed out, the criterion used under the Pigouvian approach, Pareto optimality, has tended to be regarded by the state as a license to set arbitrary standards for effluents "in the public interest." Hence, at the microeconomic level the pollution problem can be formulated in a way that is perfectly symmetrical to the depletion problem, with the emission standard replacing the natural limits on the availability of the resource.

Assume, again, that the system decomposes as in 6.10 and 6.11, where the production of noneconomic wastes is recorded in the rows of $\mathbf{B}_{22}(k)$. For a program of production in the ith process extending over k periods the problem may be written as

$$\max \Sigma_t \, q_i(t)[\underline{b}_i\mathbf{p}(t+1) - \underline{a}_i\mathbf{p}(t)][1+d_i]^{-t} \qquad t = 0, \ldots, k-1 \qquad 9.6$$

subject to

$$\Sigma_s \, q_i(s)b_{il} \leq W_l(t) \qquad s = 0, \ldots, t; \, t = 0, \ldots, k-1 \qquad 9.7$$

which states that the total quantity of emissions of the lth pollutant during the program should not exceed an upper bound, given by $W_l(t)$ in period t. Assuming, for convenience, the durability of such emissions, the Lagrangean form of the function is

$$L = \Sigma_t \, q_i(t)[\underline{b}_i\mathbf{p}(t+1) - \underline{a}_i\mathbf{p}(t)][1+d_i]^{-t} + \Sigma_t \, \psi(t)[W_l(t) - \Sigma_s \, q_i(s)b_{il}]$$
$$s = 0, \ldots, t; \, t = 0, \ldots, k-1 \qquad 9.8$$

from which, by differentiating with respect to $q_i(t)$, we can see that a necessary condition for a maximum where the constraint is binding is that

$$\underline{b}_i\mathbf{p}(t+1) = \psi(t)b_{il}[1+d_i]^{-t} + \underline{a}_i\mathbf{p}(t) \qquad 9.9$$

Hence the optimal program of production will be one in which the level of activity is such that the value of outputs in each period will be equal to the costs of all economic inputs plus the undiscounted *producer cost* of the noneconomic waste generated in that period.

Since this formulation of the optimal pollution problem is rather unusual, even though quite intuitive, it needs a word of explanation. In the depletion problem, optimization at the microeconomic level requires that the agent(s) concerned take account of the opportunity cost of a scarce but unpriced (since unproduced) resource. The value put on the resource to reflect this opportunity cost – the "shadow price," or Lagrangean multiplier in the optimization problem – is readily interpreted as a royalty equal to the user cost of the resource. In the pollution problem the agents are required to take into account the opportunity cost of producing an unpriced waste product that is expected (if $W_l < \infty$) to have adverse indirect effects on future output. The value put on the production of such pollutants is just as readily interpreted as a pollution levy equal to the producer cost. Both the pollution and the depletion problems thus center on the concept of an opportunity cost that involves lost output in the future.

What is interesting about the symmetry between the two problems is the role of the discount rate in each. In both cases the higher the discount rate, the higher the level of activity – the rate of exploitation of the depleted resource or the rate of emission of the pollutant. In the depletion problem, a low discount rate implies that more of an exhaustible resource will be left in the environment for future extraction than under a high discount rate. In the pollution problem, a low discount rate implies that less of the pollutant will be emitted in the present than under a high discount rate. The buildup of pollutants will proceed at a slower pace.

The other side of the microeconomic optimization problem in both cases is a Pigouvian collective control problem in which the same shadow prices, the royalty and the pollution levy, are the control variables. Where rights to exploit an environmental resource are granted by the collectivity to an individual agent or agents, the royalty may be claimed by the collectivity and may be manipulated to influence the rate of depletion to bring it into line with the social as opposed to the private rate of time preference. Analogously, where the rights to pollution are granted by the collectivity to individual agents, the pollution levy, a Pigouvian pollution tax, may be similarly claimed and similarly manipulated by the collectivity. It follows, therefore, that the private optimization and control problems will yield the same solution (a competitive equilibrium in a Walrasian sense will exist) only where there is no difference between the private and social discount rates (Fisher, 1981, p. 36).

9.5   The market solution and environmental equilibrium

The market solution may in fact be seen as an attempt to close the gap between social and private discount rates; partly by educating private individuals to confront the needs of the future and partly by restricting the authority of the state to impose a discount rate markedly different from that of the individual members of the community. Marglin (1963) would in fact seem to be the architect of both strands in the approach. The result is that in the market solution the limit to pollution is less and less the product of government decree and more and more the result of negotiated settlements between the parties alleged to be at either end of an external effect. Hence, we arrive at a justification for the proposition that environmental external effects on the pollution side are a function of too little market and not too much. Market information assumes such importance because a Pigouvian role for the state has been rejected.

It is worth repeating, though, that the notion that market-derived information is superior to any other is a normative judgment. The fact that it gains some support from the individualistic bias of the Pareto criterion only confirms this. Two points are at issue in deciding on the quality of market information. To get at the first, note that the realization of an outcome that is optimal from the perspectives of both individual and collectivity before and after the fact requires not only that a common rate of time preference exists, but that the respective optimization problems do in fact incorporate signals that accurately measure all the relevant variables. As was shown in Chapters 4 and 6, this is just not possible at the level of the global system, and the extent to which it is feasible at the microscopic level depends on the particular circumstances of the problem concerned. It is widely recognized, though, that it is not generally possible to approach microeconomic depletion and pollution control problems using economic instruments and expect the precise responses of a missile guidance system. But no more is it possible for individual agents to find durable solutions to the private optimization problem in the face of environmental external effects. In both cases the incompleteness of the economic signals is the problem. To that extent, the development of markets for external effects under the market solution where no markets currently exist might be expected to yield "better" results, but this only follows if there is no other mechanism for regulating the use of the resource.

The second point at issue is the question of what information is relevant to the decision-making process. This is, as we have seen, crucially dependent on the time frame of the problem, which is a function of the rate of time preference. In this connection, uncertainty and the private discount rate would seem to be related in the same way in the pollution problem as in the depletion problem. The uncertainty facing polluters is greater the less understood are the limits of tolerance of the physical system, and the greater the uncertainty, the greater the temptation to discount the future more heavily. The more the future is discounted, the fewer the effects that are relevant to the optimization problem and the fewer the data that will be sought in its solution. Decisions made on the basis of data relating to a short time frame will tend to yield more unexpected effects than those made from data relating to a longer time frame.

The anticipation of the future effects of programs of production in a far-from-equilibrium system is in large part a function of the quality of the information before the decision makers. But it is also a function of the strategy adopted to deal with uncertainty. A central argument of this essay is that economic growth in an economy-environment system subject to the conservation of mass is logically inconsistent with all but the most restrictive concepts of equilibrium. The golden paths of the long-run equilibrium growth models turn out – if I may be allowed to mix the metaphors of different modern fables – to be merely straightened versions of the yellow brick road. Illumination comes to those who tread such paths only from the unexpected surprises and novelties that crop up along the way. Decisions affecting the rate of exactions on or insertions into the environment are of necessity made under uncertainty. Since the range of future effects of present activities cannot be known, the only sure thing is that we will find the future surprising. The market solution represents an approach to the uncertainty of an evolutionary system that ultimately depends on flexibility of response, and the ability to rewrite the programs of production that are in part cause of the uncertainty. This is, after all, what the market is supposed to be good at. But there is a certain irony in this, given that the decision-making models underpinning the approach assume an omnicompetence on the part of the decision maker that makes no allowance for uncertainty. The result is that such models have to be restricted to what has been termed here the environmental short period. They have to exclude surprise. They must be myopic, ignoring the fact that myopic behavior is a magnet for unexpected effects.

CHAPTER 10

The stationary state

10.1 The stationary state in political economy

The environmental strategy behind the market solution supposes that all significant long-period problems associated with economic growth in an economy-environment system of fixed mass may be resolved in the marketplace. It supposes that economic signals generated in the course of transactions between economic agents will be sufficient to head off such global depletion and pollution disasters as those predicted by the Club of Rome. More particularly, it supposes that the negative feedbacks of the price system will ensure that rational economic agents cannot overexploit their environment. It is important to appreciate, though, that the market solution represents an historically unique environmental strategy, and an historically unique sense of rationality. It has no direct parallels in other societies. Indeed, it shares very few features with the environmental strategies of other societies.

To understand the *differentia specifica* of the market solution it is useful to look at other environmental strategies. Although this takes us beyond the bounds of the modern economy, and beyond the rationality of modern economic theory, it addresses similar issues to those raised in various modern debates about the environmental implications of economic growth. The Club of Rome debate, for example, was largely about alternative environmental strategies. The antigrowth elements in the arguments of Forrester et al. were, at the same time, positive pleas for a more quiescent approach to the management of the environment. Nor are these arguments without precedent in the economic literature. Indeed, they are implicit in the conservationism of the very old argument in favor of the stationary state.

It is important, at the outset, to distinguish the stationary state of an economy-environment system from the abstract mechanical notion of a system at rest that economics has borrowed from classical physics for use in static equilibrium analysis. The concept of the stationary state of an economy-environment system implies only the zero physical growth of the economy. It does not imply that this represents a stable equilibrium. Nor does it imply a steady state in the sense of the

141

term as it is used in capital and growth theory (where relative prices remain constant over time).

The earliest, and still the most powerful, exponent of the idea of the stationary state was John Stuart Mill, whose chapter on the stationary state in the *Principles* remains the most complete of the classical statements on the concept. Mill differed from his predecessors primarily in that he did not regard the stationary state with aversion. Whereas Adam Smith had been pessimistic about the prospects of maintaining the real incomes of workers under conditions of zero economic growth, Mill was optimistic. Smith described the stationary state as "hard" and "dull" (1970, p. 184), yet Mill saw it as "a very considerable improvement on our present condition" (1970, p. 113). What all agreed on was that, in the absence of technological change, the stationary state was the inevitable end point of economic development. According to Mill:

It must always have been seen, more or less distinctly, by political economists, that the increase of wealth is not boundless: that the end of what they term the progressive state lies the stationary state, that all progress in wealth is but a postponement of this, and that each step in advance is but an approach to it .... The richest and most prosperous countries would very soon attain the stationary state, if no further improvements were made in the productive arts, and if there were a suspension in the overflow of capital from those countries into the uncultivated or ill-cultivated regions of the earth (1970, p. 111).

The stationary state was temporarily escapable, in Mill's view, only by intensifying the exploitation of the immediate environment, through "improvements" in the "productive arts," or through expansion into new environments, "the overflow of capital."

What the stationary state meant to Mill and his predecessors was "a stationary condition of capital and population"; that is, a constant population and a fixed mass of capital. It did not imply the absence of technological change, "the industrial arts might be as earnestly and successfully cultivated," Mill argued, but only so long as technological change was directed at ends other than the accumulation of capital. In the stationary state "industrial improvements would produce their legitimate effect, that of abridging labor" (1970, p. 116).

Mill's reasons for welcoming the stationary state were essentially ethical. "I confess," he wrote, "I am not charmed with the ideal of life held out by those who think that the normal state of human beings is that of struggling to get on; that the trampling, crushing, elbowing, and treading on each other's heels, which form the existing type of social life, are the most desirable lot of human kind, or anything but the disagreeable symptoms of one of the phases of industrial progress" (1970, p. 113). These arguments have found frequent echoes in the last two decades, the strongest of which is also the most deliberate. Herman Daly's advocacy of the steady-state economy is a deliberate revival of the forgotten chapter of Mill's *Principles*. Of all the antigrowth arguments this is the most firmly and consciously rooted in Mill. Not only is Daly's definition of the steady-state identical to Mill's definition of the stationary state, the basis of Daly's concern shadows Mill's revulsion of the untrammelled effects of private self-interest in a finite world. All that Daly adds to Mill is the insights drawn from the perception of the earth as a thermodynamically closed system due to Boulding and Georgescu-Roegen.

Daly defines the steady state to be "an economy in which the total population and the total stock level of physical wealth are maintained constant at some desired levels by as 'minimal' rate of maintenance throughput" (1973, p. 152). This rather inelegant "rate of maintenance throughput" is a matter of judgment, but it is also related to the limits of tolerance of the general system. Given that any level of activity will be both waste and entropy-producing, and consequently dependent on both the absorptive capacity of the environment and the new energy flowing into the system, the sustainability of the steady state will tend to diminish with every increase in the "rate of maintenance throughput."

The necessity for the steady state follows, as Daly points out, from physical first principles. Because the global ecosystem is in a steady state, by Daly's definition, and since the human economy is a subsystem of the global system, in some time period the economy must attain a steady state. This is, of course, exactly the conclusion reached in Part I of this essay, and described in Section 4.5 as the paradox of growth. Moreover, it neatly parallels the arguments of both the classical political economists and the Physiocrats. The steady state is, in the long period, a physical necessity. The steady state is also, however, argued to be worth pursuing before it is forced upon us. Just as Mill hoped that humankind would embrace the stationary state before being compelled to do so, Daly argues that the steady state would engender a "moral growth" that would more than compensate for the physical growth that is currently the only answer to the tensions of distributional inequality.

What is interesting about this revival of Mill's stationary state is what sort of environmental strategy it implies. Mill was clear that one of his goals was to prevent the complete appropriation of the environment (for both aesthetic and moral reasons) by limiting the demands made on it. Daly's intent is similar. Without being very specific, he recommends that the key form of environmental control should come on the depletion rather than the pollution side. Depletion and pollution levels should be set to "long-run ecologically sustainable levels" by "social decision." As already indicated, just what levels appears to be as much an ethical as a physical question. "The rate at which the stock of terrestrial low entropy should be depleted is fundamentally a moral decision and should be decided on the grounds of ethical desirability (stewardship), not technological possibility or present value calculations of profitability" (1973, p. 162). This last consideration leads him to reject the notion of control via the price system. Since, he argues, physical quantities and not prices affect the ecosystem, it is ecologically safer to allow demand fluctuations to work themselves out through price shifts, rather than through changes in the rate of depletion of pollution. Hence, he advocates the use of tradable depletion quotas. Traditional Pigouvian pollution taxes are argued "to intervene at the wrong end with the wrong policy tool" (1973, p. 166).

We will return to the principles behind these recommendations later. Enough has been said, though, to indicate that the central property of the environmental strategy associated with the stationary state, at least in the minds of modern economists, is the regulation of the level at which the economic system is allowed to exploit its environment. To get a sense of the generality of such an environment strategy, we may now consider those precapitalist economic systems which, more than any other historical systems, have come closest to attaining the stationary state.

10.2   "Cybernetic savages": the stationary state in primitive economics

One of the most striking features of the primitive economies is the historical longevity of both the technologies applied and their enabling institutions. It has, for example, been reported that many Asiatic village communities employed the same technology for over two millennia (Krader, 1975). I have argued elsewhere (Perrings, 1985) that this reflects the collective regulation of capacity utilization in primitive economies to minimize excess demand for environmental resources. It is not the product of the sloth or ignorance of individuals.

The dominant microeconomic explanation of the performance of primitive economies is that associated with Chayanov (1966) who claimed that peasant households differed from capitalist enterprises in that the objective function of the former was not profit but utility maximization. The peasant household thus tended to produce up to the point at which the marginal utility of income was just equal to the marginal disutility, the drudgery, of work. In consequence, the intensity of household labor in primitive economies tended to be inversely related to its productive capacity, implying that excess capacity above that required to produce necessities was a normal feature of such economies.

The weight of evidence on the point, however, appears to favor a different explanation. The same slack in the system has been investigated in a range of historical circumstances by anthropologists, and it is generally argued to reflect not the preferences of individual agents but the existence of collective constraints on individual behavior. So Sahlins (1974) argues that social cohesion in the community demands that the level of activity taken to be the norm must be attainable by the majority of households. Hence, households that are more productive than the average, by reason, for instance, of their position in the family cycle, will tend to produce below capacity to avoid creating social tension. The existence of norms implies some sort of social consensus about the appropriate level of activity, and this implies a collective decision – however taken. Nash (1967), too, emphasizes the role of the collectivity, arguing that while individuals within primitive economies tend to have the same "motive for gain" as economic man, they are constrained by their social institutions to produce below capacity. Godelier goes even further in his description of primitive economies. In noting that the "social structure" systematically underutilizes available factors of production, he argues that this reflects "the *conscious control* that 'primitive' or ancient societies habitually exercise over themselves," to meet various social objectives, including the sustainability of the ecosystem (1972, p. 290). Godelier suggests that this is perfectly rational behavior, though the rationality of such systems should not be mistaken for the individualistic rationality of "economic man."

The suggestion that the underutilization of capacity reflects the decision of the collectivity to operate at a level of activity that minimizes stress on the environment implies that environmental signals play a significant role in determining economic activity. This, in turn, implies an environmental strategy that, unlike the market solution, regulates the level of economic activity according to a set of environmental indicators. The strategy may thus be thought of as approaching a homeostatic control mechanism, without implying that the economy-environment system is strictly controllable.

The controllability of the environment is, in fact, an issue that has already been canvassed by anthropologists. The title of this section is drawn from Jonathen Friedman's entertaining defense of his criticism

of the notion that Maring rituals homeostatically regulate Maring society in response to changing environmental signals. Friedman attacks
the identification of ritual as homeostatic in primitive societies on two
levels. The first is the weaker of the two. A ritual like pig slaughter
among the Maring, he argues, reduces the strain on the environment
of an excessive pig population only incidentally. It is not the primary
intention of those undertaking the ritual. Pig slaughter is symbolically
linked not to the relief of the environment, but to a range of human
relations of power and prestige. The fact that a particular human society adopts rituals that help it to refrain from destroying itself by
destroying its environment in the short term does not, he argues, necessarily imply a planned response to some environmental signal. This
line of attack, though, is hardly persuasive, since it makes no difference
if the agents seeking to control a particular system believe the inner
workings of that system to be different to what they are, so long as the
end result is desired. The Montgolfier brothers believed that smoke
made their balloons "fly"; it is irrelevant that they were mistaken.
What is important is that they wished to fly and took action that had
that effect. The same applies to the rituals of primitive societies. It
makes no difference whether the sustainability of a society is conceptualized in terms of relations of power and prestige or of optimal pig
densities. All that matters is that rituals exist that guarantee the one by
working on the other.

More persuasively, Friedman argues that in the long term empirical
evidence simply contradicts the notion of the planned regulation of
human societies. Although he acknowledges that "it is conceivable that
some social systems might . . . oscillate between the same values or
limits," he argues that "social evolution has not exhibited such long-
run stability. As social systems tend to be of an accumulative nature,
stable 'cybernetic' cycles are contained within long term secular trends
leading to crises, breakdowns and reorganization" (1979, p. 269).

Friedman's authority for this last statement is Prigogine's analysis
of the behavior of far-from-equilibrium "dissipative" structures in
contact with their environment. Prigogine argues that such structures
may exhibit a degree of local stability only so long as they do not
infringe the limits imposed by an environment that is itself composed
of similarly dissipative structures. It follows from this that the idea of
homeostatic control may indeed have some validity, but only as a
description of human behavior in the interstices of an environmental
flux beyond human control. "Stability," as Friedman puts it, "is not
the miraculous outcome of self control but the result of the existence
of degrees of freedom within larger systems" (1979, p. 268).

In Prigogine's work the stability and control of systems are indissolubly linked: "the instability threshold of a system marks the point where the "control" of the system through the limiting conditions . . . has broken down completely" (1977, p. 329). Hence, the local stability of some system is conceivable so long as it is controllable within the limits imposed by its environment. Stability implies controllability, and noncontrollability implies instability. The problem with the notion of the homeostatic control of primitive societies is not that the mechanisms of control are unconscious, in the sense that they are shrouded in mysticism and ritual, but that it implies an unchanging and therefore predictable or "knowable" environment. To the extent that the environmental limits are predictable, then a system may be homeostatically controllable. But if the limits imposed by the environment are not predictable, the system will not be homeostatically controllable. It will be compelled to mutate; to adapt to change in its environment (see, for example, Norgaard, 1984).

The environmental strategies of the primitive economies are, in fact, better thought of as strategies designed to minimize the potential for environmental surprise. Such strategies are no more capable of exercising complete control over the environmental effects of economic activity than the market solution, but by minimizing the stress that is placed on the environment by human activity, they minimize the potential for unanticipated future effects. They are strategies for dealing with uncertainty by other means than direct discounting, although it should be added that reducing uncertainty in this manner involves, implicitly, much lower rates of time preference than under the market solution.

One final point is that the fewer the feedback effects of human activities involving either exactions on or insertions into the environment, the fewer the strains on the internal social structure of human economies. For this reason, a homeostatic interpretation of the environmental strategies of primitive economies – as regulators of the level of exactions on or insertions into the environment – provides valuable insights into both their institutional longevity and their technological conservatism. But it also highlights their susceptibility to unanticipated environmental change, since the habit of non-innovation makes it very difficult to react to change in the environmental parameters of the system. The regulation of levels of capacity utilization to minimize environmental stress in fact emphasizes the uncontrollable and unobservable aspects of the environment. The environment may not be tamed through the application of residuals generated within the economy. Hence the "cybernetic savage" aims not to displease the gods who control the environment, and acts always on the assumption that those gods are at best capricious and at worst downright malevolent.

10.3   The stationary state of an evolutionary system

The stationary state of a closed system does not, it should now be clear, mean that it will be technologically time invariant for the simple reason that the stationary state will not eliminate the raison d'être of systemic change – the existence of residuals or spare capacity. The same conclusion, however, follows from the laws of thermodynamics. Recall that under the Second Law an isolated system (not receiving energy from its environment) is characterized by the fact that its entropy will increase up to the point at which it is in thermodynamic equilibrium and energy flows cease. The entropy of an isolated system cannot decrease. On the other hand, a closed system (receiving energy from across its boundaries) will still experience the same irreversible increase in the entropy of its mass, but will be able to avoid the oubliette of thermodynamic equilibrium by tapping the energy flowing into the system from the outside. Since an increase in entropy implies the progressive degradation of available energy, it follows that an isolated system in which agents perform useful work on its resources will converge to thermodynamic equilibrium or "heat death." A closed system, by contrast, offers the option of degrading the available energy of the system itself, or of tapping the energy crossing the boundaries of the system. The implications of this are important.

Consider these comments on non-isolated systems by Prigogine and Stengers (1977):

In these systems variation in entropy is not only linked to processes within the system, as in the isolated systems, but also to the energy and matter [if the system is open] flows between the systems and the environment. The mere consideration of entropy is no longer sufficient to determine the system's behavior, as the second principle sets no conditions on entropy variation linked to the exchanges with the environment. In the non-isolated systems, the decisive magnitude is no longer entropy but *entropy production,* i.e., the variation in unit time of the entropy linked to the processes *inside* the system. The second principle requires the production of entropy to be either positive or zero. In a non-isolated system, irreversible processes can be taking place permanently, and entropy production be different to zero, while an interaction with the environment has the effect of maintaining the system in a state different to that of equilibrium (1977, pp. 326–27).

To each closed system there corresponds a state of minimum entropy production consistent with the inflows of energy from outside. The level of activity at such a state is then entirely dependent on the level of energy inflows. It is this minimum entropy stationary state that Daly refers to.

Notice, though, that the minimun entropy stationary state is not necessarily stable. The agents of closed, far-from-equilibrium systems do have freedom of maneuver with respect to the organization of energetic and material processes. It is Prigogine's argument that the time path of far-from-equilibrium closed systems may be characterized by a sequence of dissipative structures, each founded on excess entropy production and each the unique outcome of a particular set of physical and energetic conditions. The properties of such structures depend on the time behavior of both of the antecedent structures and the relation of those antecedent structures to the environment. There are no fixed patterns of change.

The same element of choice and the myriad of essentially unreproducible energy and material flows to which it gives rise have also been used by Georgescu-Roegen in his attempts to persuade economists of the entropic bounds to the apparently limitless freedom of human economies to exploit their environment. The Second Law, the entropy law, is, he points out, the only physical law that does not predict quantitatively. It specifies only the direction of change in entropy. Useful work raises entropy; it says nothing about the magnitude of entropy increase nor about the entropic pattern. At the process level, the Second Law requires only that entropy increase in a process exploiting its environment should be more than compensated by entropy increases in the environment (Georgescu-Roegen, 1976). At the global level, however, it dictates that the system will evolve from one state to the next, in which each stage in the evolutionary process is irreversible. Once a particular configuration of resources is lost it will never be repeated. This is as true of the stationary state as of any other.

Even more telling against the concept of a stable stationary state, however, is that any system dependent on exhaustible resources will always be biting into and changing its environment. Both energy and, Georgescu-Roegen claims, matter are continuously degraded through use, and so continuously pass from available to unavailable form. Just as not all energy in the system may be converted into mechanical work, so too not all matter in the general system is available for transformation into usable goods. "Certainly," Georgescu-Roegen admits, "the whole planet is made of matter, but the argument based on this [that we will never run out of material resources] ignores the fact that, just like the thermal energy of the earth, not all terrestrial matter is in available form. Matter also continuously degrades into an unavailable form" (1979, p. 1032). Moreover, just as the Second Law of thermodynamics precludes the reversibility of energetic processes, so too are many material transformations irreversible for all practical purposes.

To use one of Georgescu-Roegen's own examples, it is notionally possible to reassemble the molecules of a bottle of ink sprinkled over the Atlantic, but for all practical purposes the act is an irreversible one. Consequently, the change in the material transformations of the general system caused by the disposal of residuals either randomly or by design creates a sequence of new and different states, in which the only constant is the mass of the sum of all resources. The material transformations of one moment will never be reproduced at a later time.

The inference is that technological change – reflected in a change in the composition of the system's resources – is both evolutionary and irreversible. Like time, it is a one-sided phenomenon. A nonequilibrium closed system inexorably moves from a sequence of past known states to a different sequence of future unknown states. Every change in the technology of systems opens the door to further change. Hence, we are led to the conclusion that while physical first principles indicate the necessity of the stationary state, so too do they indicate that any system away from thermodynamic equilibrium will be time variant. The environmental strategy that rests on a form of homeostatic control does no more than minimize the potential surprise or uncertainty associated with economic activity. It does not eliminate it.

10.4   The role of the collectivity

What is really at issue in the quiescent environmental strategies is not the growth orientation of the economy. The sustainability of a given system is undoubtedly more secure under a low growth than a high growth strategy, but this is only interesting if one is concerned with the sustainability of the system. What marks off the quiescent environmental strategies is the role of the collectivity in translating the collective perception of intertemporal equity into rules of behavior and their supporting institutions. If this has been confounded with the anti-growth ideas of the proponents of quiescent environmental strategies, it is because the one is a function of the other. Underpinning the anti-growth ideas of most proponents of the stationary state is an egalitarianism that is fundamentally antithetical to the present-oriented individualism of the market solution. It demands that the collectivity restrain the narrow selfishness of the current members of society in the interests of members yet to come.

Daly's conviction of the need to exercise stewardship over the rate of depletion of resources, his mistrust of the use of private discount rates, and his insistence on the need to deal with distributional matters directly and not via the rate of growth, are exactly what was at issue in

Marglin's rejection of the Pigouvian approach to environmental management. It is the Pigouvian state's guardianship of the interests of future generations that is set aside by Marglin. It is the economic libertarians' conviction of the sovereignty of present individuals that is rejected by Daly.

Randers and Meadows are even more explicit about the centrality of the social rate of time preference:

We see that adherence to the short-term objective function avoids very simply all trade-offs of current benefits for future costs. Of course, man is left with the more usual trade-offs that affect people alive today – for instance, the choice between denying the firm upstream freedom to dump waste in the river and denying those who live downstream pure drinking water. But conflicts within the short term are not our concern here, because we *do* have mechanisms in our society to resolve conflicts between people alive today.

We do *not* have, however, mechanisms or even moral guidelines for resolving conflicts between the population of the present and the people of the future. ... So basically there is only one question in the impending global crisis. Should we continue to let our actions be guided by the short-term objective function, or should we adopt a long term perspective? In other words, what time horizon should we use when comparing the costs and benefits of current actions? (1973, pp. 300–301).

The presumption that the appropriate time horizon is one that encompasses intergenerational issues leads to the conviction that it is the collectivity and not individuals within it that should determine the environmental strategy adopted by society. As Myrdal (1975) points out, though the price signals generated by the market solution may indeed have the effect of changing the actions of private individuals charged with the management of environmental resources, there is no reason to believe that these signals will be unambiguous given the multiple layers of information contained in market prices, and therefore no reason to believe that they will generate appropriate responses. They will certainly not touch the discount rate. Indeed, for Myrdal the central problem in environmental management is to circumvent the ignorance, shortsightedness, and narrowmindedness of individuals accustomed to acting solely in their own short-term interests (1975, pp. 232–33).

To the extent that these views can be interpreted in the language of intergenerational welfare theory they imply the application of a Rawlsian or egalitarian criterion. This is certainly how Dasgupta and Heal (1979) interpret Randers and Meadows' statements. We have already seen that the egalitarian criterion is inconsistent with the existence of a positive social rate of time preference, and it would seem to be a reasonable interpretation of the views of Randers and Meadows that they reject the positive discounting of the future. But there is another even more interesting implication of the egalitarian criterion, and that is that it is inconsistent with the Pareto criterion. In 1965 Diamond showed that a continuous social welfare function might either be Paretian or treat different generations equally, but that no continuous social welfare function exists that is at once Paretian and intertemporally egalitarian. If one insists on the formulation of a social welfare function to allow the ordering of states consistent with the collective sense of intertemporal justice, then one has to forgo either the Pareto criterion or the equal treatment of generations. Under the market solution the equal treatment of generations is the casualty.

The justification for admitting the principle of discounting in this context, and so the justification for the unequal treatment of generations, is argued to be the uncertainty of the continued existence of the species in the future. As Dasgupta and Heal, citing Sidgwick, put it: "one might find it ethically reasonable to discount future utilities at positive rates, not because one is myopic, but because there is a positive chance that future generations will not exist" (1979, p. 262). To those in favor of a more quiescent environmental strategy, an ethic that justifies behavior that increases the uncertainty of future existence, on the grounds that some cosmic cataclysm has always been possible anyway, might appear to be remarkably self-serving. It is cold comfort to learn that such an ethic underpins the use of the individualistic Pareto criterion.

What marks off the environmental strategies associated with the stationary state is that the well being of the collectivity and not of the individuals within it is paramount. Hence, a constant refrain in the arguments of those who have been concerned about the long-period environmental effects of economic activity has been the importance of the role of the collectivity in suppressing the current activities of individual agents that threaten to damage the system in the future. In stark contrast to the market solution, such environmental strategies seek to maintain the collective control over the allocation of environmental resources that is authorized by common property. They attempt to deny the primacy of the private perspective on time reflected in interest and profit rates, and they seek to negate the sovereignty of the individual under the Pareto criterion.

CHAPTER 11

Conclusions

11.1 Closing the mind with the model

What marks off the primitive economies and their watchers, the anthropologists, is an acute awareness of the interaction between the economy and its environment. The observation that primitive economies exist within the limits imposed by a constantly changing environment occurs time and time again in the anthropological literature. Yet the environmental constraints to economic activity warrant only passing mention in the economic literature. The environment made its appearance in the classical works of Malthus, Smith, and Ricardo only obliquely – through the land scarcity that underlies the theory of diminishing returns. But if the classical political economists had little regard for the environmental constraints to growth, their successors seem to have none at all. Despite the fact that the scarcity of resources was enshrined as the raison d'être of the theory of resource allocation by Robbins (1932), it has disappeared as a meaningful concept from modern dynamic general equilibrium theory. Indeed, as we have already seen, theories resting on the strong environmental assumption simply wish away the environment altogether, while theories resting on the weak environmental assumption suppose that a string of substitutable resources of one sort or another are available in limitless supply.

The difference is that anthropologists are first of all observers. Their primary concern is the description of real human societies. Economics, and theoretical economics in particular, has increasingly adopted different concerns. Theoretical economics has become what Kornai calls a "logical mathematical" as opposed to a real science. That is, it comprises "a theorem or body of theorems logically deducible from a set of mutually consistent axioms" as opposed to "a systematic description of the essential interrelations between the variables of reality" (1972, p. 9). The ultimate test of truth in a real science is whether or not its propositions correspond to reality. In the logical-mathematical sciences truth implies only that the deductions from a given set of axioms are logically correct. Yet as Kornai points out, economics can

153

be nothing more than an irrelevant intellectual experiment unless it addresses itself to the world as it is and not as the economist would have it to be.

Both the general equilibrium models of Walras and Neumann are true in a logical-mathematical sense, but neither can be said to be true in a real sense so long as their axiomatic foundations are not rooted in the reality they seek to explain. It is not enough that each incorporates some aspect of reality such as the well-recognized empirical law of supply and demand, or the existence of growth over time. An economy is very much more than a closed clearing house or an automatously compounding amoeba-like system of processes, and to reduce it to either is pure perversion. The problem with such theories is not, as Kornai admits, their axiomatic treatment, but that the axioms fail to reflect reality.

If the bounds of the theory are artificially prescribed by initial assumptions that have no bearing on the real world, the theory is akin to a laboratory experiment. The economists' assumptions and the chemists' test tube similarly prescribe the bounds within which the experiment takes place. It is legitimate to argue the general relevance of the result if and only if nothing of importance has been omitted in those bounds, and if no other results are possible within their confines. But many key results of economic theory do depend on the way in which a model is bounded. The modern theory of duality is a prime example. The formal duality between equilibrium price and quantity vectors provides justification for the view that it is sufficient to know the former to know the latter, yet even in its less dogmatic forms, the theory of duality claims too much. Where the weak environmental assumption is diluted to admit environmental surprises, for example, it is argued that if real world prices are not in fact good indicators of the state of the physical system due to either uncertainty (ex ante) or external effects (ex post), they can be made so by making formal allowances for risk.

Though Neumann's work was instrumental in establishing the duality between price and quantity vectors in a model of general economic equilibrium, the argument that data on the physical system are thereby redundant is of more recent origin. It is associated with the development of a microeconomic approach to duality that traces itself back to Shephard's (1953) proof of the duality between cost and production functions in the context of a cost-minimizing problem. The implications of Shephard's conclusions have been teased out by McFadden. The result, he argues, "establishes that the cost function contains all the information necessary to reconstruct the structure of production possibilities. It is in a sense a 'sufficient statistic' for the technology" (1978, p. 19).

Recall, though, that the duality between price and quantity vectors at the level of the system is an equilibrium condition. Consequently, the duality of price and quantity vectors presupposes all those assumptions necessary for the convergence of the general system. McFadden's remark will hold for the general system only if it satisfies either the assumptions of free disposal and free gifts and is on the equilibrium path, or if it is assumed that the environment does not exist, implying a system of production of commodities by means of commodities. Since these assumptions may not be satisfied in a closed economy-environment system, it follows that the price and quantity vectors in such a system will not be dual to one another. The price system will not contain all relevant information about the physical system. In terms of its ability to convey information on the environment, the price system suffers from the same limitations as any more direct measure of the residuals generated by the economy, such as stock levels. That is, the maximum rank of the observability matrix is identical, whether the observers are prices or stock levels.

Opening the models of economic systems to the effects that follow from their interaction with the environment has implications that are just as startling as the opening of systems in the natural sciences. In the far-from-equilibrium thermodynamics of Prigogine referred to at intervals throughout this book, the flows of energy and matter between a referent system and its environment generate a chaotically evolving sequence of unstable structures. This essay has not needed the force of the Second Law of thermodynamics to show the inevitability of irreversible and unpredictable change in the technology and enabling institutions of human economies, but the Second Law nevertheless lends powerful support to its arguments. We have seen that change in the economic variables of a jointly determined economy-environment system is sufficient to compel change in the material transformations of the environment, and that this will react upon the material transformations of the economy. Change in the material transformations of the general system caused by the disposal of residuals either randomly or by design creates a sequence of new and different states, in which the only constant is the mass of the sum of all resources. There is no stable equilibrium state for any economy, though there may be temporary checks to change in both technology and enabling institutions.

Economic systems may achieve a degree of local stability by minimizing stress on the environment, but the aggressively expansive capitalist economy necessarily generates feedback effects that accelerate the pace of change in the material transformations of the general system. Since this is the negation of equilibrium, the concept of a relatively stable expansion path for an economy in a jointly determined economy-environment system is nothing less than a contradiction in terms: a contradiction that can only be avoided by closing both mind and model to the realities of the environmental repercussions of growth.

11.2   The value of market signals

What, then, is the value of the signals of the economy, the prices of economic resources? If the concept of attainable equilibrium is displaced, and if the general system is unobservable through the weights attaching to the valorized resources, what are the implications of using prices as a basis for decision making? These questions are posed against a backdrop of the increasing dominance of the market solution to the problem of the environment, and so the increasing confidence of those who argue that market signals contain all the information we need to know about the physical world.

This book has argued that the price system cannot be regarded as an adequate set of observers of the environment and that it cannot be assumed that only irrelevant environmental effects are ignored. Indeed, since the price system is limited both by the time perspectives of the economic agents and by the presence of uncertainty, it cannot be supposed to be proof against adverse future effects of present actions. Moreover, this is true regardless of the market-clearing qualities of any particular set of prices. In other words, market-clearing prices are no better in this respect than nonmarket clearing prices. By the arguments of Section 4.2, it is true that if market clearance means that no residuals exist to be disposed of as waste in the environment, then market-clearing prices will minimize the environment repercussions of the corresponding resource allocation decisions. But market clearance means only that there are no residuals on the market floor. There is no economic waste. Only if the market floor corresponds to the general physical system will the two coincide. There is no reason at all to suppose that a set of prices that leaves agents with unsold stocks at the end of the period will have more or less long-period effects than a set of prices that clears those stocks. In fact, the lessons of the primitive economies indicate exactly the opposite. Historically, as we have seen, societies seeking to minimize the environmental effects of economic activity have deliberately refrained from the full utilization of capacity. If market-clearing prices ensure full capacity utilization in all processes, then the environmental impacts associated with the disposal of noneconomic wastes may be higher than those associated with the disposal of economic wastes in the case of nonmarket-clearing prices.

The reason for this, as we have seen, is that real uncertainty is an increasing function of the level of economic activity. The greater the stress placed on the environment through exactions and insertions, the greater the potential surprises among the unobserved environmental effects. The efficiency of the market solution thus depends either on a time perspective that fully discounts such surprises or on a set of prices that fully anticipates them. The latter can only be assured by appeal to the sophism of probabilistic uncertainty. But, as has been argued here, the accommodation of environmental effects through the pricing for risk is essentially irrelevant. It misunderstands the essential nature of the problem. The nature of change in a technologically dynamic general system is quintessentially unknowable: the problem is not one of balancing the probability of one or other determinate outcome. The system evolves through a sequence of states, the range of which is not predictable on the basis of economic data. In fact, resource allocation decisions taken on the basis of a given set of prices in an economy-environment system will have entirely indeterminate long-period effects. Although a particular allocation may be optimal in terms of the short-period objectives of the agents of the economy, it will generate a progressive sequence of changes in the material transformations of the general system that will ensure that the same allocation will be sub-optimal in terms of the same objectives in future periods. In short, the price system is not a good basis for determining whether one allocation is better than another in terms of its long-period implications. The intertemporal efficiency of the market solution in an uncertain world depends on an ever-shortening time perspective.

11.3 Economy, environment, history

It should be clear that one of the greatest sources of instability in the global system is our perspective on time. It is worth pointing out, therefore, that a time perspective involves not only the future, but also the past. History matters. The knowledge of a process can only be the knowledge of its history. In terms of the model discussed in this essay it is trivially true that the state of the system in any one period is explicable only in terms of its evolution from some arbitrary initial state. Even under the powerful protective assumptions of free goods, free disposal, and zero technological change, the present state of an automatous system is given by a sequence of changes from some initial disequilibrium state. If we do not know what that initial state was, or how it evolved, we cannot explain the present state. We can only describe it. We cannot guess at its future potential – we can only discount it.

But history matters in another, more practical sense. Recall that the distinction between crucial and noncrucial activities is that crucial activities are historically unique while the noncrucial ones have historical precedents. In other words noncrucial activities are similar in whole or in part to activities previously undertaken in the system. There accordingly exist a number of observations on which to construct a probability distribution for all possible outcomes associated with the type of activity in question. In crucial activities, on the other hand, there exist no observations on which to construct a probability distribution for their outcomes. Noncrucial activities may therefore be said to be subject to risk, crucial activities to uncertainty. It is, therefore, only to the extent that activities are noncrucial that they support probabilistic evaluation. Only the historical precedents for activities with noncrucial elements enable us to say something about the range and distribution of possible outcomes.

The task of history is accordingly enormous. We need to know how the technology of the general system and the enabling institutions change with each round of residuals disposals, and what the effect of such changes is on the signals informing the behavior of all active agents in the system. The initial state may be succeeded by any one of a number of possible though unknown and unknowable states, depending on the relations of dominance and subordination within the general system. As one subsystem becomes dominant at the expense of its environment, so that environment is squeezed into a new form, and this in turn reacts upon the form of the now dominant subsystem. As Prigogine has argued in a more general context:

When several dissipative states are accessible beginning from an unstable state, no *macroscopic* description enables one to predict which fluctuation is going to occur, or towards which mode of functioning the system is going to tend .... A structure produced by a *succession* of amplified fluctuations can thus only be understood by reference to its past; no description of its physico-chemical state at any given moment can explain its functioning; and this past, interwoven with unpredictable events, will soon have to be considered as unique and unreproducible. For what reason should we thus avoid saying that a dissipative structure is properly the product of an individual *history*? ... "mutations" may affect certain units, or other types of units may be introduced which set up and imply a new type of relation between the system's constituents. This thus leads to actual competition between the different possible modes of functioning of the system. The mutants, or intruders, initially present in only small numbers, will be eliminated and "orthodox" functioning preserved except when their presence causes this functioning to become unstable. In this case, instead of being destroyed, they will multiply and the whole system will adopt this new mode of functioning at the cost of the destruction of those that no longer play any role in it (1977, p. 330).

It may be noted, in passing, that this bears a striking resemblance to Marx's view of the process of social change. On the one hand, we have the classical Marxian contradiction of antiquated social structures seeking to retain cohesion in the face of changes in the forces of production; to crush the threat posed by the social mutants thrown up as a response to change in the conditions of production. On the other, we have the overthrowing of the old order as the contradiction can no longer be contained, as the pressures to change become too great to accommodate. Certainly, there is nothing to support the prophetic element in Marx, but this one would not expect. What Prigogine adds, of crucial importance to the arguments of this essay, is the notion that social structures may be tipped over the "instability threshold" both by internal contradictions and "as a result of a new interactions with the environment" (1977, p. 330).

In the case of an economic system that is jointly determined with its environment, the history of the economy and the history of its environment are interlinked, as change in one creates new forms in the other. Though it is not, in general, possible to predict what those new forms are going to be from a knowledge of the history of the system, it is possible to get a feel for the convergence of any particular system on the limits imposed by its environment. It is accordingly possible to say which of a number of subsystems will first run into a binding environmental constraint; which will find least resistance to its expansion; which will be able to resist the expansion of other subsystems and which will not.

In the history of economic systems these questions determine the rationality of any particular system. What is and what is not rational in a particular system depends on what is and what is not feasible. If it is not now feasible for a particular economy to sustain a particular strategy in the face of a binding environmental constraint, then it will not now be rational to adopt such a strategy. On the other hand, this does not mean either that it will never be rational to adopt such a strategy, or that, once adopted, such a strategy will always be rational. As Godelier has reminded us, there is no unique or absolute rationality. What is rational today may be irrational tomorrow, what is rational in one society may be irrational in another (1972, p. 317). The *Limits to Growth* was a crude and rather blunt attempt to test the rationality of current depletion strategies by looking at the convergence of the economic system on its environmental constraints. That it was methodologically flawed is less important than the fact that it gave tacit recognition to the importance of the past evolution of the system in the search for its future. A sustainable environmental strategy implies a time perspective that is careless of neither future interests nor past experience.

11.4   Principles for a sustainable environmental strategy

To the extent that the problem of time perspectives in the evolution of environmental strategies has been canvassed by economists, the consensus would be that it remains a matter of ethics, of normative judgment. The choice of rates of time preference can be reduced to a judgment about intertemporal equity, in which economists allegedly have no role beyond the analysis of the effects of various intertemporal welfare functions. Whether, like Marglin (1963), one employs what may be termed the historical-democratic principle to elevate the rights of historically located individuals to impose their own time perspective on society, or, like Rawls (1971), to apply what may be termed the original-democratic principle which asks individuals to choose from behind a "veil of ignorance" as to their true status in place and time, one makes a moral judgment. Although the historical-democratic principle leads to discounting and the unequal treatment of different generations, the original-democratic principle involves the equal treatment of different generations. Choice of the former favors the market solution, choice of the latter does not.

What is not clear, however, is what is implied by an egalitarian principle for an alternative strategy in a world in which neither Mill's stationary state nor the primitive economy have much appeal. The historical-democratic principle leads very directly to a decentralized decision-making process. The original-democratic principle appears to lead nowhere. It is, after all, hardly reasonable to suppose that real decisions could or should be abstracted from the historical circumstances in which they are made. Nor is it reasonable to expect every economic agent to have the strength of imagination to satisfy Ramsey, Pigou, or Harrod on the question of discounting. But there are environmental principles that are consistent with a more intertemporally egalitarian approach than that implied by the historical-democratic principles, which do lead into familiar modes of decision making.

The principle of common property

The first of these, the principle of common property, requires that title to all environmental resources should rest with the collectivity. The private use of such resources should be on the basis of usufructual rights only. In other words, private agents might be authorized to exploit environmental resources, but only on terms and conditions that reflect the interests of the collectivity. There are, of course, obvious difficulties to be overcome in advocating a principle of this sort. The pronounced ideological bias against collective property in much of the Western world is one, although there is little that I can do to counter this. The widely held view that common property engenders inefficiency is another. Indeed, this view is the basis for an equally pronounced but professional bias against common property among economists. Because it notionally rests on defined theoretical foundations, however, it is a bias that ought to be amenable to argument.

The point was made in Section 6.3 that it is not common property per se that is the source of difficulty. What Hardin has referred to as "the tragedy of the commons" (1968) is the product of unconstrained private use of common property and is not inherent in the concept of common property. Hardin is partly guilty for the fact that his paper has caused confusion on this point. By defining the tragedy to follow "the day when the long-desired goal of social stability becomes a reality," he implied that the inefficiencies of common property exist whether or not the use of that property is regulated. But this is misleading. Hardin's story is a simple one. Assume that a common pasture exists that is underutilized by graziers, as a result of "tribal wars, poaching, and disease." Suppose that these constraints on its utilization are now removed. What is the incentive to each grazier to add an extra beast to the pasture? Given that each grazier receives the whole of the sale price of the extra beast, but shares the loss in average animal weight as a result of overgrazing with all other graziers, there is every incentive for individual graziers to keep adding beasts to the pasture. Hence, Hardin's conclusion: "freedom in the commons brings ruin to all." The crucial word here is freedom. The overexploitation of common resources follows only if access to those resources is unregulated. But common and open access property are not synonymous. Not all property in the public domain is unregulated in its use. Historically, very few socially important and collectively owned resources have been unregulated. Social stability has depended on collective control of the use of such resources. The problem of the overexploitation of resources not in private ownership is a problem that has existed only in the absence of collective control. The mass slaughter of the American buffalo in the last century, or the overgrazing of the Sahel in this one, are typical examples of the rape of an unprotected environment. In both cases, the mechanisms for ensuring the sustainability of the resource were either destroyed or severely weakened. In most cases, however, we are led to conclusions diametrically opposite to those reached by Hardin. Wherever common property has been collectively regulated, it has if anything led to the underutilization and not the exhaustion of environmental resources. Collective interest in the sustainability of production turns out to be a much more powerful incentive to conserve a given set of resources than private interest in the maximization of the income derived from exploiting resources wherever they are located.

The common property principle applies to all resources not privately possessed: that is, all resources whose production is not controlled by private agents. Because they are unobservable through the price system, such resources are the main source of environmental external effects, and this is so whether they are in private ownership or not. The user or producer cost of exactions on (or insertions into) the processes yielding such resources is unknowable. We may, however, at least monitor such costs through the regulation of the terms of usufructs granted to private individuals. An additional point, worth noting, is that the absolute right over resource allocation implied by the concept of private property generally employed by economists is no more than a convenient abstraction from a world in which most property rights are conditional on the use of the resource in some specified way. Effectively, many notionally absolute private property rights are usufructual. Proprietors do not have the right of destruction of their property, but are institutionally constrained to use that property in what is recognized to be a socially responsible way. The common property principle does no more than regularize this for a particularly important class of resources.

The important consideration here is that in a time-varying, uncertain world, it is desirable to retain sufficient collective control over the allocation of resources exacted from the environment to ensure that the interests of future generations are safeguarded both by appropriate pricing of access to such resources and by limitations on the range of potential uses. A time-dependent usufructual right is equivalent to a lease on the collective property, which has the advantage over private property that it provides a means for the collectivity to conduct regular reviews of the activity in question. Tradable usufructs of fixed term would allow the redetermination of categories of use without sacrificing either the efficiency of markets in the usufructs or the right of the collectivity to prohibit activities that generate undesirable effects. The common property principle may be seen as a means of amalgamating the assumptions underpinning the theory of royalties in the depletion problem, and of Pigouvian taxes in the pollution problem. The extractive industries have long come to terms with the existence of collective property in mineral resources that have none of the usual properties of public goods, while the nonexclusiveness and nonrivalness of effects on the pollution side have long accustomed governments to act as if the affected property was in the public domain. Its primary target, however, is the generation of institutional flexibility in the face of uncertainty without recourse to ruinously high rates of time preference.

The principle of private accountability

A second principle that is consistent with a degree of intergenerational equity is what may be called the principle of private accountability. It is the principle that individual agents using environmental resources in a given economic process should be constrained to recognize the time distance of that process from other potentially affected processes. It was argued in Chapter 2 that the isolation of particular subsystems in an indecomposable global system represents the myopic decomposition of that system; the application of a time perspective that is short enough to rule out all but the most immediately affected processes from the relevant set. The historical-democratic principle suggests that the choice of time perspective, and so the range of effects consciously considered in the decision-making process, should be left entirely up to the individual. As a matter of principle, however, it would seem reasonable for the collectivity to prohibit such myopic decomposition of an interdependent system. More particularly, it would seem reasonable to prohibit the arbitrary, private determination of the commercial equivalents of the statute of limitations on the effects of private activities through the discounting of the future.

The principle is partly recognized in the definition of external effects, but it is largely ignored in the market solution to the problem. Recall that the market solution supposes that markets in the external effects will develop spontaneously whenever the exclusiveness and rivalness of property permit it, and wherever the benefits to be gained from trading in markets for external effects outweigh the costs of setting them up. Since it is very sensitive to the quality of information, the structure of power, and other factors of importance in the small numbers bargaining problem, and since it accepts the primacy of the private perspective on time, however, the market solution does no more than open up the possibility that individual agents will be held accountable for some of their actions.

The problem here is that wherever the private rate of time preference is higher than the social rate of time preference, then even if private and social attitudes to risk are the same, it will be socially optimal to internalize external effects by the assignment of property rights to those effects only where there is no time distance between the affected processes. If a delay exists in the transmission of external effects, it will never be socially optimal to leave the settlement of disputes over external effects in private hands. The nonequivalence of market and non-market solutions to the problem of external effects vanishes only in the purely static Walrasian analysis (cf. Seneca and Taussig, 1984, and Fisher, 1981).

A wide range of mechanisms currently exists for the social control of external effects due to both pollution and depletion caused by private activities, of which price or fiscal incentives and quantitative restrictions are the most important. However, the emphasis of this essay on the role of time and uncertainty in the realization of external effects makes one instrument of special interest: the environmental bond. The use of bonds in environmental management is now new. Indeed, it has been recommended for some time wherever direct observation and detection of environmental damage are impossible or extremely difficult (cf. Baumol and Oates, 1975, 1979). By this criterion the environmental bond is a natural measure for dealing with the crucial aspects of activities with potential environmental external effects.

The modern treatment of environmental bonds appears to date from two contributions by Mill (1972) and Solow (1971), who separately advanced the idea of a materials-use fee to be levied on specified environmental resources at a rate equal to "the social cost to the environment if the material were eventually returned to the environment in the most harmful way possible" (Solow, 1971, p. 502). The fee was thus seen to be equivalent to the refundable deposit long used to encourage the recycling of potentially environmentally harmful products, and was designed to provide an incentive for private users of environmental resources to dispose of the waste in a socially preferred way. It has since become common to use the materials-use fee as clean-up insurance in a wide range of cases. The two things to note about the fee are that it is concerned with the existence of social costs occurring *after* the economic usefulness of an environmental resource has passed and is related to the *worst case* – the most harmful method of waste disposal. Recall that there is, by definition, insufficient information on which to determine the expected value of the external effects of crucial activities. Recall, too, no algorithm exists by which to determine what is effectively a premium for social insurance against losses due to environmental external effects when those external effects are uncertain. In the face of complete ignorance, the most harmful method of disposal can only be interpreted as the maximum conjectured loss caused by the external effects of a particular program of activity.

It may be noted, in parentheses, that whether the maximum conjectured loss or maximum conjectured gain due to external effects is used to inform the collective response will depend on the form of the relevant social welfare function. For social welfare functions of the normal form – continuously differentiable concave functions – the relevant measure will be the maximum conjectured loss. For strictly convex functions it will be the maximum conjectured gain. The reason is that the risk aversion of strictly concave social welfare functions focuses attention on conjectured losses, while the risk avidity of strictly convex social welfare functions focuses attention on conjectured gains. Ordinarily, therefore, it will be the maximum conjectured loss that is relevant.

An environmental bond associated with the use of environmental resources as either inputs or the receptacle for wastes should be a monotonically increasing function of the present social value of the maximum conjectured losses in all affected processes over all relevant periods, the function to reflect the risk aversion of the society concerned. The intuition is clear on this. The greater the maximum conjectured loss, the more care should be taken in constructing a reliable data set on which to found decisions. Maximum conjectured losses that are insignificant do not warrant extensive initial investigation. Maximum conjectured losses that are catastophic demand a major research effort. The present social value of the maximum conjectured loss is thus a measure of the value to society of conducting research into the possible outcomes of activities with potential environmental external effects.

It is, at the same time, the first stage in the sequential determination of an environmental bond. If the size of a bond on the use of a particular resource is determined by maximum conjectured losses associated with that resource, it will be sensitive to research that improves understanding of at least the range of possible outcomes. A bond established in ignorance in the first period may be reduced (increased) in subsequent periods if research shows the initial conjecture to be unduly pessimistic (optimistic). Wherever a sequential process leaves an irreducible residuum of uncertainty, however, the present social value of the maximum conjectured remaining loss indicates the appropriate value of the environmental bond required to indemnify society against that loss.

It should be noted that the present social value of the maximum conjectured loss may or may not be equal to the materials-use fee attached to Solow's "most harmful" means of waste disposal. The reason is that the existence of uncertainty is only one of the circumstances in which a bond may be indicated. The nonexistence of an enforceable contractual obligation on the user of environmental resources to perform in predictable way is the justification for requiring a bond. Where the purchaser of a resource is free to dispose of it in any of a number of ways, each with different known effects, the materials-use fee provides an incentive to adopt the least socially harmful method of disposal. In such circumstances the appropriate value of the bond is the present social expected value of the external effects, and not the present social value of the maximum conjectured loss. Where a program of activity is subject to the social evaluation of its external effects, every tax or subsidy is contingent on a particular set of actions. So, for example, a program of activity for which a range of possible waste disposal methods exists would be taxed on the basis of the method of disposal agreed to by the agents concerned.

An environmental bond set at the present social value of the maximum conjectured loss due to the external effects of a program of activity is designed to indemnify society against effects which, because they are uncertain, cannot be specified contractually. In this sense it is identical to the materials-use fee. What determines the value of the bond in each case is, however, different. The expected value of external effects in noncrucial activities is a sufficient datum to establish a premium for social insurance against those effects; the present social value of the maximum conjectured loss due to external effects in crucial activities is the only datum available to a risk averse society.

What is interesting about this view is that it involves a role for the collectivity quite different from that posted by the market solution. Wherever the set of future outcomes and the probability distribution of those outcomes is known, the collectivity is required to insure its members against the possibility of future social damage resulting from the external effects of present activities. Wherever the set of future outcomes is not known, the collectivity is required to name and hold the indemnity demanded of the individual agents responsible for potential future damage. Only those activities with minimal or immediate external effects may, in this view, be appropriately accommodated by the allocation of private property rights in the effects.

Of course, neither of these principles – the common property principle and the private accountability principle – can ensure that future generations will not be bequeathed a wasteland. History is pockmarked with examples of collective folly, and the current obsession with the curious doctrine of safety in the threat of annihilation does not bode well for the future. Indeed, there is a cruel irony in the fact that Sidgwick's original justification for discounting – uncertainty even as to the continued existence of human beings – is given real meaning by a doctrine that allegedly guarantees our future. By reintroducing the role of the collectivity into the regulation of the use of domestic resources, however, and by denying the historical-democratic right of individuals to act as if the system decomposed in their favor, the two principles might help to ensure against the myopic and cavalier approach to the accommodation of environmental uncertainty of the market solution.

References

Abraham-Frois, G. and Berrebi, E. (1979) *Theory of Value, Prices and Accumulation*, Cambridge, Cambridge University Press.

Aoki, M. (1976) *Optimal Control and System Theory in Dynamic Economic Analysis*, Amsterdam, North-Holland Publishing.

Arrow, K. J. and Hurwicz, L. (1972) "An Optimality Criterion for Decision-Making Under Ignorance," in C. F. Carter and J. L. Ford (eds.), *Uncertainty and Expectations in Economics*, Clifton, N.J., Augustus M. Kelly, pp. 1–11.

Ayres, R. U. (1972) "A Materials-Process-Product Model," in A. V. Kneese and B. T. Bower (eds.), *Environmental Quality Analysis*, Baltimore, Johns Hopkins Press, pp. 35–67.

Ayres, R. U. and Kneese, A. V. (1969) "Production, Consumption and Externalities," *American Economic Review*, 59, pp. 282–97.

Bator, F. (1958) "The Anatomy of Market Failure," *Quarterly Journal of Economics*, 72, pp. 351–79.

Baumol, W. J. (1972) "On Taxation and the Control of Externalities," *American Economic Review*, 62, pp. 307–22.

Baumol, W. J. and Oates, W. E. (1975) *The Theory of Environmental Policy*, Englewood Cliffs, N.J., Prentice-Hall.

(1979) *Economics, Environmental Policy, and the Quality of Life*, Englewood Cliffs, N.J., Prentice-Hall.

Beckerman, W. (1972) "Economists, Scientists, and Environmental Catastrophe," *Oxford Economic Papers*, 24, pp. 237–44.

Bender, B. (1975) *Farming in Prehistory*, London, John Baker.

Boulding, K. E. (1966) "The Economics of the Coming Spaceship Earth" in H. Jarrett (ed.), *Environmental Quality in a Growing Economy*, Baltimore, Johns Hopkins Press, pp. 3–14.

Brooks, D. P. and Andrews, P. W. (1974) "Mineral Resources, Economic Growth, and World Population," *Science*, 5, July, pp. 13–19.

Burmeister, E. (1980) *Capital Theory and Dynamics*, Cambridge, Cambridge University Press.

Carvalho, F. (1983) "On the Concept of Time in Shacklean and Sraffian Economics," *Journal of Post-Keynesian Economics*, 6, 2, pp. 265–80.

Chayanov, A. V. (1966) "On the Theory of Non-Capitalist Systems," in D. Thorner and B. Kerblay (eds.), *On the Theory of Peasant Economy*, Homewood, Ill., Irwin.

Ciriacy-Wantrup, S. (1952) *Resource Conservation: Economics and Policies,* Berkeley, University of California Press.

Ciriacy-Wantrup, S. and Bishop, R. (1975) "Common Property as a Concept in Natural Resource Policy," *Natural Resources Journal,* 15, 4, pp. 713–27.

Coase, R. H. (1960) "The Problem of Social Costs," *Journal of Law and Economics,* 3, pp. 1–44.

Cumberland, J. H. (1966) "A Regional Inter-Industry Model for Analysis of Development Objectives," *Regional Science Association Papers,* 17, pp. 65–94.

Dahlman, C. J. (1979) "The Problem of Externality," *Journal of Law and Economics,* 22, pp. 141–62.

(1980) *The Open Field System and Beyond,* Cambridge, Cambridge University Press.

Daly, H. E. (1968) "On Economics as a Life Science," *Journal of Political Economy,* 76, pp. 392–406.

(1973) "The Steady State Economy: Toward a Political Economy of Biophysical Equilibrium and Moral Growth," in *Toward a Steady State Economy,* San Francisco, W. H. Freeman, pp. 149–74.

D'Arge, R. C. (1972) "Economic Growth and the Natural Environment," in A. V. Kneese and B. T. Bower (eds.), *Environmental Quality Analysis,* Baltimore, Johns Hopkins Press, pp. 11–34.

Dasgupta, P. S. and Heal, G. M. (1979) *Economic Theory and Exhaustible Resources,* Cambridge, Cambridge University Press.

Davidson, P. (1982) "Rational Expectations: A Fallacious Foundation for Studying Crucial Decision-making Processes," *Journal of Post-Keynesian Economics,* 5, 2, pp. 182–98.

Debreu, G. (1959) *Theory of Value: An Axiomatic Analysis of Economic Equilibrium,* Cowles Foundation Monograph 17, New Haven, Yale University Press.

Demsetz, H. (1966) "Some Aspects of Property Rights," *Journal of Law and Economics,* 9, pp. 61–70.

(1967) "Toward a Theory of Property Rights," *American Economic Review,* 57, pp. 347–59.

Diamond, P. A. (1965) "The Evaluation of Infinite Utility Streams," *Econometrica,* 33, pp. 170–77.

Dolan, E. G. (1976) *The Foundations of Modern Austrian Economics,* Kansas City, Sheed and Ward.

Duijn, J. J. van (1983) *The Long Wave in Economic Life,* London, George Allen and Unwin.

Feige, E. L. and Blau, D. M. (1980) "The Economics of Natural Resource Scarcity and Implications for Development Policy and International Cooperation," in P. Dorner and M. A. El-Shafie (eds.), *Resources and Development,* London, Croom Helm, pp. 109–48.

Fisher, A. C. (1981) *Resource and Environmental Economics,* Cambridge, Cambridge University Press.

Fisher, A. C. and Krutilla, J. V. (1975) "Resource Conservation, Environmental Preservation, and the Rate of Discount," *Quarterly Journal of Economics,* 89, pp. 358–70.

Forrester, J. W. (1971) *World Dynamics,* Cambridge, Mass., Wright Allen Press.

Freeman, H. (1965) *Discrete Time Systems,* New York, Wiley.

Friedman, J. (1979) "Hegelian Ecology: Between Rousseau and the World Spirit," in P. Burnham and R. F. Ellen (eds.), *Social and Ecological Systems,* London, Academic Press, pp. 253–70.

Gandolfo, G. (1971) *Mathematical Methods in Economic Dynamics,* Amsterdam, North-Holland.

Gantmacher, F. R. (1959) *Applications of the Theory of Matrices,* New York, Interscience.

Georgescu-Roegen, N. (1971) *The Entropy Law and the Economic Process,* Cambridge, Mass., Harvard University Press.

(1973) "The Entropy Law and the Economic Problem," in H. Daly (ed.), *Toward a Steady State Economy,* San Francisco, W. H. Freeman, pp. 37–49.

(1976) *Energy and Economic Myths: Institutional and Analytical Economic Essays,* Cambridge, Mass., Harvard University Press.

(1977) "Matter Matters, Too," in K. D. Wilson (ed.), *Prospects for Growth: Changing Expectations for the Future,* New York, Praeger, pp. 293–313.

(1979) "Energy Analysis and Economic Evaluation," *Southern Economic Journal,* 45, 4, pp. 1023–58.

Godelier, M. (1972) *Rationality and Irrationality in Economics,* New York, Monthly Review Press.

Gordon, H. S. (1954) "The Economic Theory of a Common Property Resource," *Journal of Political Economy,* 75, pp. 274–86.

Hardin, G. (1968) "The Tragedy of the Commons," *Science,* 162, pp. 1243–48.

Harrod, R. F. (1948) *Towards a Dynamic Economy,* London, Macmillan.

Herfindahl, O. C. and Kneese, A. V. (1974) *Economic Theory of Natural Resources,* Columbus, Ohio, Charles E. Merrill.

Herskovits, M. J. (1940) *The Economic Life of Primitive Peoples,* New York, Alfred Knopf.

Hotelling, H. (1931) "The Economics of Exhaustible Resources," *Journal of Political Economy,* 39, pp. 137–75.

Jevons, W. S. (1906) *The Coal Question,* edited by A. W. Flux, London, Macmillan (3rd edition).

Kapp, W. (1969) "On the Nature and Significance of Social Costs," *Kyklos,* 22, 2, pp. 334–47.

Kemp, M. V., Long, N. V. and Shimomura, K. (1984) "The Problem of Survival: A Closed Economy," in M. C. Kemp and N. V. Long (eds.), *Essays in the Economics of Exhaustible Resources,* Amsterdam, North Holland.

Kindleberger, C. P. (1965) *Economic Development,* New York, McGraw-Hill (2nd edition).

Kneese, A. V., Ayres, R. U. and d'Arge, R. C. (1970) *Economics and the Environment,* Washington, Resources for the Future.
(1974) "Economics and the Environment: A Materials Balance Approach," in H. Wolozin (ed.), *The Economics of Pollution,* Morristown, N.J., General Learning Press.
Knight, F.H. (1921) *Ris, Uncertainty and Profit,* Boston, Houghton-Mifflin.
Koopmans, T. C. (1960) "Stationary Ordinal Utility and Impatience," *Econometrica,* 28, pp. 287–309.
Kornai, J. (1972) *Anti-Equilibrium,* Amsterdam, North-Holland.
Kornai, J. and Martos, B. (1981) "Vegetative Control," in J. Kornai and B. Martos (eds.), *Non-Price Control,* Amsterdam, North-Holland.
Krader, L. (1975) *The Asiatic Mode of Production,* Assen, Van Gorcum.
Lange, O. (1971) *Political Economy,* Oxford, Pergamon Press.
Leibenstein, H. (1975) *Economic Backwardness and Economic Growth,* New York, Wiley.
Leontief, W. W. (1941) *The Structure of the American Economy, 1919–1929: An Empirical Application of Equilibrium Analysis,* Cambridge, Mass., Harvard University Press.
(1970) "Environmental Repercussions and the Economic Structure: An Input-Output Approach," *Review of Economics and Statistics,* 52, pp. 262–71.
(1971) "Theoretical Assumptions and Nonobserved Facts," *American Economic Review,* 61, pp. 74–81.
Lewis, T. R. (1976) "Monopoly Exploitation of an Exhaustible Resource," *Journal of Environmental Economics and Management,* 3, pp. 198–204.
Lipnowski, I. F. (1976) "An Input-Output Analysis of Environmental Preservation," *Journal of Environmental Economics and Management,* 3, pp. 205–14.
Lotka, A. J. (1956) *Elements of Mathematical Biology,* New York, Dover.
Makarov, V. L. and Rubinov, A. M. (1977) *Mathematical Theory of Economic Dynamics and Equilibria,* New York, Springer-Verlag.
Malthus, T. R. (1970) *An Essay on the Principles of Population,* edited by A. Flew, Harmondsworth, Penguin Books.
Marchetti, C. (1980) "Society as a Learning System: Discovery, Invention and Innovation Cycles Revisited," *Technological Forecasting and Social Change,* 18, pp. 267–68.
Marglin, S. A. (1963) "The Social Rate of Discount and the Optimal Rate of Investment," *Quarterly Journal of Economics,* 77, pp. 95–112.
Marx, K. (1954, 1974) *Capital, I, III,* London, Lawrence and Wishart.
(1971) *A Contribution to the Critique of Political Economy,* London, Lawrence and Wishart.
(1973) *Grundrisse,* Harmondsworth, Penguin.
McFadden, D. (1978) "Cost, Revenue and Profit Functions," in M. Fuss and D. McFadden (eds.), *Production Economics: A Dual Approach to Theory and Applications,* 1, Amsterdam, North Holland.

Meade, J. E. (1952) "External Economies and Diseconomies in a Competitive Situation," *Economic Journal,* 62, pp. 54–67.

(1973) *The Theory of Economic Externalities,* Geneva, Institut Universitaire de Haute Etudes Internationales.

Meadows, D. H., Meadows, D. L., Randers, J. and Behrens, W. (1972) *The Limits to Growth,* New York, Universe Books.

Mill, E. S. (1972) *Urban Economics,* Glenview, Ill., Scott, Foresman.

Mill, J. S. (1970) *Principles of Political Economy,* edited by D. Winch, Harmondsworth, Penguin Books.

Mises, L. von (1949) *Human Action: A Treatise on Economics,* London, William Hodge.

Mishan, E. J. (1971) "The Postwar Literature on Externalities: An Interpretive Essay," *Journal of Economic Literature,* 9, pp. 1–28.

Morgenstern, O. and Thompson, G. L. (1976) *Mathematical Theory of Expanding and Contracting Economies,* Lexington, D. C. Heath.

Morishima, M. (1964) *Equilibrium, Stability, and Growth: A Multisectoral Analysis,* Oxford, Oxford University Press.

Myrdal, G. (1975) *Against the Stream,* New York, Vintage Books.

Nash, M. (1967) "The Social Context of Economic Choice in a Small Society," in G. Dalton (ed.), *Tribal and Peasant Economies,* Austin, University of Texas Press.

Neumann, J. von (1945–6) "A Model of General Equilibrium," *Review of Economic Studies,* 13, 1, pp. 1–7.

Norgaard, R. B. (1984) "Coevolutionary Agricultural Development," *Economic Development and Cultural Change,* 32, 3, pp. 525–46.

O'Brien, D. P. (1975) *The Classical Economists,* Oxford, Oxford University Press.

Pasinetti, L. I. (1981) *Structural Change and Economic Growth: A Theoretical Essay on the Dynamics of Wealth of Nations,* Cambridge, Cambridge University Press.

Perrings, C. (1985) "The Natural Economy Revisited," *Economic Development and Cultural Change,* 33, 4, pp. 829–50.

(1986a) "Conservation of Mass and Instability in a Dynamic Economy-Environment System," *Journal of Environmental Economics and Management,* 13, pp. 199–211.

(1986b) "Income Redistribution and Labour Surplus in the Classical Theory of Labour Migration," *The Manchester School,* 54, 3, pp. 283–97.

Pigou, A. C. (1932) *The Economics of Welfare,* London, Macmillan (4th edition).

Prigogine, I. (1971) "Time, Structure and Entropy," in J. Zeman (ed.), *Time in Science and Philosophy,* Amsterdam, Elsevier, pp. 89–100.

Prigogine, I. and Stengers, I. (1977) "The New Alliance, Part 1 – From Dynamics to Thermodynamics: Physics, the Gradual Opening to the World of Natural Processes," *Scientia,* pp. 319–31; "Part 2 – An Extended Dynamics: Towards a Human Science of Nature," *Scientia,* pp. 643–53.

Ramsey, F. P. (1928) "A Mathematical Theory of Saving," *The Economic Journal*, 38, pp. 543–59.

Randers, J. and Meadows, D. (1973) "The Carrying Capacity of our Global Environment: A Look at the Ethical Alternatives," in H. E. Daly (ed.), *Toward a Steady-State Economy*, San Francisco, W. H. Freeman.

Rawls, J. (1971) *A Theory of Social Justice*, Cambridge, Mass., Harvard University Press.

Rendel, J. M. (1968) "The Control of Development Processes," in E. T. Drake (ed.), *Evolution and Environment*, New Haven, Yale University Press.

Repetto, R. and Holmes, J. (1983) "The Role of Population in Resource Depletion in Developing Countries," *Population and Development Review*, 9, 4, pp. 609–32.

Review of Economic Studies (1974) *Symposium on the Economics of Exhaustible Resources.*

Ricardo, D. (1951) "The Principles of Political Economy and Taxation," in P. Sraffa (ed.), *The Works and Correspondence of David Ricardo, 1*, Cambridge, Cambridge University Press.

Robbins, L. (1932) *An Essay on the Nature and Significance of Economic Science*, London, Macmillan.

Rostow, W. W. (1960) *The Stages of Economic Growth: A Non-Communist Manifesto*, Cambridge, Cambridge University Press.

Sahlins, M. (1974) *Stone Age Economics*, London, Tavistock Press.

Salisbury, R. (1962) *From Stone to Steel*, Cambridge, Cambridge University Press.

Scitovsky, T. (1954) "Two Concepts of External Economies," *Journal of Political Economy*, 62, pp. 143–51.

Seneca, J. J. and Taussig, M. K. (1984) *Environmental Economics*, London, Prentice-Hall.

Shackle, G. L. S. (1949) *Expectation in Economics*, Cambridge, Cambridge University Press.

(1955) *Uncertainty in Economics*, Cambridge, Cambridge University Press.

(1961) *Decision, Order and Time in Human Affairs*, Cambridge, Cambridge University Press.

(1970) *Expectations, Enterprise and Profit*, London, George Allen and Unwin.

(1972) *Epistemics and Economics*, Cambridge, Cambridge University Press.

Shephard, R. W. (1953) *Cost and Production Functions*, Princeton, Princeton University Press.

Sidgwick, H. (1890) *The Methods of Ethics*, London, Macmillan.

Smith, A. (1970) *An Inquiry into the Nature and Causes of the Wealth of Nations*, edited by A. S. Skinner, Harmondsworth, Penguin Books.

Smith, V. L. (1977) "Control Theory Applied to Natural and Environmental Resources," *Journal of Environmental Economics and Management*, 4, pp. 1–24.

Solow, R. M. (1971) "The Economist's Approach to Pollution Control," *Science*, 173, pp. 498–503.

174   References

(1973) "Is the End of the World at Hand?" in A. Weintraub et al. (eds.), *The Economic Growth Controversy*, London, Macmillan, pp. 39–61.

(1974) "Intergenerational Equity and Exhaustible Resources," *Review of Economic Studies Symposium*, pp. 29–45.

Sraffa, P. (1960) *Production of Commodities by Means of Commodities*, Cambridge, Cambridge University Press.

Stiglitz, J. E. (1974) "Growth with Exhaustible Resources: the Competitive Economy," *Review of Economic Studies Symposium*, pp. 139–52.

Tsukui, J. and Murakami, Y. (1979) *Turnpike Optimality in Input-Output Systems*, Amsterdam, North Holland.

Turnovsky, S. J. (1970) "Turnpike Theorems and Efficient Economic Growth," in E. Burmeister and A. R. Dobell, *Mathematical Theories of Economic Growth*, London, Macmillan, pp. 311–51.

Victor, P. A. (1972) *Pollution, Economy and Environment*, London, George Allen and Unwin.

Walsh, V. and Gram, H. (1980) *Classical and Neoclassical Theories of General Equilibrium*, Oxford, Oxford University Press.

Walras, L. (1973) *Elements of Pure Economics*, translated by W. Jaffe, Homewood, Ill., Irwin.

Weintraub, A. et al. (eds.) (1973) *The Economic Growth Controversy*, London, Macmillan.

Wonham, W. M. (1967) "On Pole Assignment in Multi-Input Controllable Linear Systems," *IEEE Transactions on Automatic Control*, AC 12, 6, pp. 660–65.

Index